GRE®

General Test

Vocabulary Building Flashcards

Staff of Research & Education Association

Research & Education Association
61 Ethel Road West
Piscataway, New Jersey 08854

Vocabulary-Building Flashcard Book
for the GRE® General Test

Printed in the United States of America

Library of Congress Control Number 2005927025

International Standard Book Number 0-87891-170-7

Vocabulary-Building Flashcards for the GRE® General Test

What they're for and how to use them

GRE test experts all agree that building a powerful "GRE" vocabulary is the single most important way you can raise your score on the Verbal Ability and Analytical Writing sections of the test. This book contains **900** flashcards of the most frequently used words on the GRE General Test.

Learning and remembering 900 words is not an easy task, especially if many of these words are new to you. This unique flashcard book is designed to help you in your quest. Each page presents the flashcard word with space to write in your definition of the word. On the flip side of each page you'll find the correct definition of the word, its part of speech (adjective, verb, etc.), and sample sentences using the word in context.

It's a three-step learning process:

1. See the word.

2. Write in your definition.

3. Flip the page over and compare your definition to the correct one.

You will also find that flashcards in a book have several advantages over flashcards in a box. You don't have to cope with hundreds of loose cards. Whenever you want to study, you can just open the book and get going.

Take this book along with you everywhere since there are a lot of words to study and the book is ready to use whenever you are.

Best to start now — test day is drawing near!

Questions

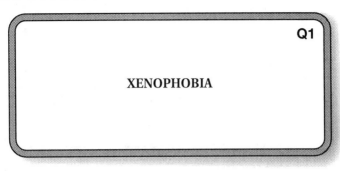

Q1

XENOPHOBIA

*Your Own Answer*_____

_____

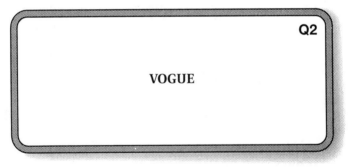

Q2

VOGUE

*Your Own Answer*_____

_____

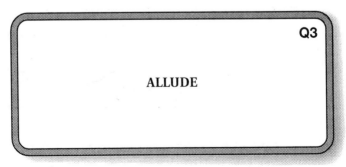

Q3

ALLUDE

*Your Own Answer*_____

_____

Correct Answers

A1

n.—fear of foreigners

Xenophobia kept the townspeople from encouraging any immigrants to move into the neighborhood.

A2

n.—modern fashion

Women's magazines advertise the clothing they believe to be in **vogue**.

A3

v.—to refer indirectly to something

Without stating that the defendant was an ex-convict, the prosecutor **alluded** to the fact by mentioning his length of unemployment.

Questions

Q4

APPOSITE

*Your Own Answer*_____

_____

Q5

STOKE

*Your Own Answer*_____

_____

Q6

GUFFAW

*Your Own Answer*_____

_____

Correct Answers

A4

adj.—suitable; apt; relevant

Without reenacting the entire scenario, the situation can be understood if **apposite** information is given.

A5

v.—to feed fuel to; especially a fire

With the last embers dying, he **stoked** the fire one more time.

A6

n.—boisterous laughter

With the **guffaw** of the boisterous crowd, the comedian was assured of his success.

Questions

Q7

TRUNCATE

*Your Own Answer*_____

Q8

TEDIOUS

*Your Own Answer*_____

Q9

REDUNDANT

*Your Own Answer*_____

Correct Answers

A7

v.—to shorten by cutting

With the football game going into overtime, the show scheduled to follow it had to be **truncated**.

A8

adj.—time-consuming; burdensome; uninteresting

Counting all the rubber bands in the box proves to be a **tedious** affair.

A9

adj.—superfluous; exceeding what is needed

With millions of transactions at stake, the bank built a **redundant** processing center on a separate power grid.

Questions

Q10

RELEGATE

*Your Own Answer*_____

_____

Q11

CALLOW

*Your Own Answer*_____

_____

Q12

ECONOMICAL

*Your Own Answer*_____

_____

Correct Answers

A10

v.—to banish; to put to a lower position

With Internal Affairs launching an investigation into charges that Officer Wicker had harassed a suspect, the officer was **relegated** to desk duty.

A11

adj.—being young or immature

With his **callow** remark, the young man demonstrated he wasn't up to the job.

A12

adj.—not wasteful; thrifty

With her **economical** sense, she was able to save the company thousands of dollars.

Questions

Q13

ACCEDE

*Your Own Answer*_____

_____

Q14

TRANSPIRE

*Your Own Answer*_____

_____

Q15

PETTY

*Your Own Answer*_____

_____

Correct Answers

v.—to comply with; to consent to

With defeat imminent, the rebel army **acceded** to hash out a peace treaty.

v.—to take place; to come about

With all that's **transpired** today, I'm exhausted.

adj.—unimportant; of subordinate standing

With all of the crime in the world, stealing bubble gum is considered **petty** theft.

Questions

Q16

PLACATE

*Your Own Answer*_____

Q17

CRAVEN

*Your Own Answer*_____

Q18

GENERIC

*Your Own Answer*_____

Correct Answers

A16

v.—to appease or pacify

With a soothing voice and the promise of a juicy steak, the trainer **placated** the escaped lion so that it wouldn't hurt anyone.

A17

n.—coward; abject person

While many fought for their rights, the **craven** sat shaking, off in a corner somewhere.

A18

adj.—common; general; universal

While **generic** drugs are often a better value, it is always a good idea to consult your doctor before purchasing them.

Questions

Q19

SERRATED

*Your Own Answer*_____

Q20

PUNGENT

*Your Own Answer*_____

Q21

ARABLE

*Your Own Answer*_____

Correct Answers

A19

adj.—having a saw-toothed edge

While camping, the family used a **serrated** band saw to cut firewood.

A20

adj.—sharp; stinging

When the refrigerator door opened, the smell of lemons was **pungent**.

A21

adj.—suitable (as land) for plowing

When the land was deemed **arable**, the farmer decided to plow.

Questions

Q22

JUNCTURE

*Your Own Answer*_____

Q23

WELTER

*Your Own Answer*_____

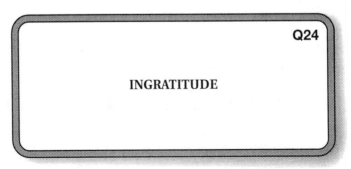

Q24

INGRATITUDE

*Your Own Answer*_____

Correct Answers

A22

n.—critical point; meeting

When the gas changed into a liquid, they sensed that they'd come to a critical **juncture** in their experimentation.

A23

n.—a confused mass; turmoil

When the emergency alarm sounded, a **welter** of shivering office workers formed in the street as people evacuated the site.

A24

n.—ungratefulness

When she failed to send a thank-you card, her friend took it as a sign of **ingratitude**.

Questions

Q25

COMPATIBLE

*Your Own Answer*_____

Q26

VITAL

*Your Own Answer*_____

Q27

VAUNTED

*Your Own Answer*_____

Correct Answers

adj.—in agreement with; harmonious

When repairing an automobile, it is necessary to use parts **compatible** with its make and model.

adj.—important; spirited

When in a foreign country, a passport is a **vital** piece of paperwork to have at all times.

v.—to boast

When her son was accepted to college, she **vaunted** his success to everyone.

Questions

Q28

SOLACE

*Your Own Answer*_____

Q29

YORE

*Your Own Answer*_____

Q30

SUCCUMB

*Your Own Answer*_____

Correct Answers

A28

n.—hope; comfort during a time of grief

When her father passed away, she found **solace** amongst her friends and family.

A29

n.—former period of time

When he sees his childhood friends, they speak about the days of **yore**.

A30

v.—to give in; to yield; to collapse

When dieting, it is difficult not to **succumb** to temptation.

Questions

Q31

SALIENT

*Your Own Answer*_____

_____

Q32

UNPRECEDENTED

*Your Own Answer*_____

_____

Q33

ECCENTRIC

*Your Own Answer*_____

_____

Correct Answers

A31

adj.—noticeable; prominent

What's **salient** about the report is its documentation of utter despair in the heartland of the richest nation on Earth.

A32

adj.—unheard of; exceptional

Weeks of intense heat created **unprecedented** power demands, which the utilities were hard pressed to meet.

A33

adj.—odd; peculiar; strange

Wearing polka dot pants and a necklace made of recycled bottle tops is considered **eccentric**.

Questions

Q34

DOCILE

*Your Own Answer*_____

Q35

DISENTANGLE

*Your Own Answer*_____

Q36

PEDESTRIAN

*Your Own Answer*_____

Correct Answers

adj.—manageable; obedient; gentle

We needed to choose a **docile** pet because we hadn't the patience for a lot of training.

v.—to free from confusion

We need to **disentangle** ourselves from the dizzying variety of choices.

adj.—mediocre; ordinary

We expected the meal to be exceptional, but it was just **pedestrian**.

Questions

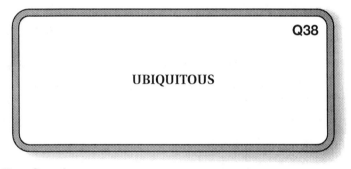

Q37

AMELIORATE

*Your Own Answer*_____

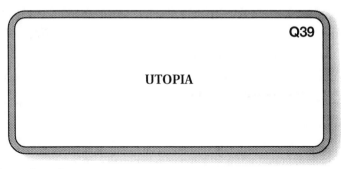

Q38

UBIQUITOUS

*Your Own Answer*_____

Q39

UTOPIA

*Your Own Answer*_____

Correct Answers

A37

v.—to improve or make better

We can **ameliorate** the flooding problem by changing the grading.

A38

adj.—omnipresent; present everywhere

Water may seem **ubiquitous**, until a drought comes along.

A39

n.—imaginary land with perfect social and political systems

Voltaire wrote of a **utopia** where the streets were paved with gold.

Questions

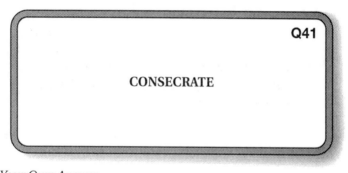

Q40

QUANDARY

*Your Own Answer*_____

Q41

CONSECRATE

*Your Own Answer*_____

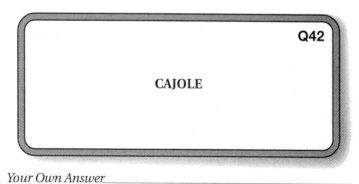

Q42

CAJOLE

*Your Own Answer*_____

Correct Answers

A40

n.—dilemma

Tristan and Elizabeth were caught in a **quandary**: Should they spend Thanksgiving with his parents or hers?

A41

v.—to sanctify; to make sacred; to immortalize

To make the new statue worthy of worship, it had to be **consecrated** by the priest.

A42

v.—to coax with insincere talk

To **cajole** the disgruntled employee, the manager coaxed him with lies and sweet talk.

Questions

QUARANTINE

*Your Own Answer*_____

_____

Q44

PERIPHERAL

*Your Own Answer*_____

_____

Q45

DECOROUS

*Your Own Answer*_____

_____

Correct Answers

A43

n.—isolation of a person or persons to prevent the spread of disease

To be sure they didn't bring any contagions back to Earth, the astronauts were put under **quarantine** when they returned.

A44

adj.—marginal; outer

Those are **peripheral** problems; let's look at the central challenge.

A45

adj.—showing decorum; propriety; good taste

This movie provides **decorous** refuge from the violence and mayhem that permeates the latest crop of Hollywood films.

Questions

Q46

MACERATE

*Your Own Answer*_____

Q47

AUGMENT

*Your Own Answer*_____

Q48

COMMODIOUS

*Your Own Answer*_____

Correct Answers

A46

v.—to soften by steeping in liquid (including stomach juices)

They placed her foot in the solvent to **macerate** the cement she had stepped in.

A47

v.—to increase or add to; to make larger

They needed more soup so they **augmented** the recipe.

A48

adj.—spacious and convenient; roomy

They need a **commodious** apartment to fit all their furniture.

Questions

MEANDER

*Your Own Answer*_____

TAUT

*Your Own Answer*_____

CONTENTIOUS

*Your Own Answer*_____

Correct Answers

A49

v.—to go aimlessly
They **meandered** through the woods for the afternoon.

A50

adj.—stretched tightly
They knew a fish was biting because the line suddenly became **taut**.

A51

adj.—quarrelsome
They hate his **contentious** behavior because every suggestion they give ends in a fight.

Questions

Q52

TREK

*Your Own Answer*_____

Q53

VENUE

*Your Own Answer*_____

Q54

LUMINOUS

*Your Own Answer*_____

Correct Answers

A52

v.—to make a journey

They had to **trek** through the dense forest to reach the nearest village.

A53

n.—location

They had always had their holiday party in the town hall; after ten years they were ready for a change of **venue**.

A54

adj.—emitting light; shining; also enlightened or intelligent

They found their way through the darkness by heading toward the **luminous** object in the distance.

Questions

Q55

GIBBER

*Your Own Answer*_____

_____

Q56

VALANCE

*Your Own Answer*_____

_____

Q57

CONNOISSEUR

*Your Own Answer*_____

_____

Correct Answers

A55

v.—to speak foolishly

They did not want him to represent their position in front of the committee since he was prone to **gibbering** when speaking in front of an audience.

A56

n.—short drapery hanging over the window frame

They decided to hang a floral **valance** over the kitchen window.

A57

n.—expert; authority (usually refers to a wine or food expert)

They allowed her to choose the wine for dinner since she was the **connoisseur**.

Questions

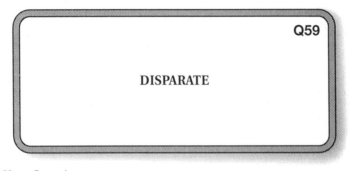

Q58

DISSENT

*Your Own Answer*_____

Q59

DISPARATE

*Your Own Answer*_____

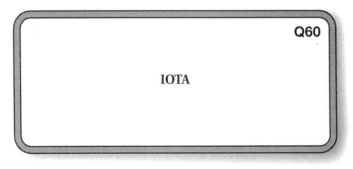

Q60

IOTA

*Your Own Answer*_____

Correct Answers

v.—to disagree; to differ in opinion

They agreed that something had to be done, but **dissented** on how to do it.

adj.—unequal; dissimilar; different

They came from **disparate** backgrounds, one a real estate magnate, the other a custodian.

n.—a very small piece

There wasn't one **iota** of evidence to suggest a conspiracy.

Questions

Q61

SUBTLETY

*Your Own Answer*_____

Q62

DISCORD

*Your Own Answer*_____

Q63

PLETHORA

*Your Own Answer*_____

Correct Answers

n.—propensity of understatement; so slight as to be barely noticeable

There was no **subtlety** in the protest; each person carried a sign and yelled for civil rights.

n.—disagreement; lack of harmony

There was **discord** amidst the jury; therefore a decision could not be made.

n.—a superabundance

There was a **plethora** of food at the royal feast.

Questions

Q64

DISPARITY

*Your Own Answer*_____

Q65

INDIFFERENT

*Your Own Answer*_____

Q66

CONTIGUOUS

*Your Own Answer*_____

Correct Answers

n.—difference in form, character, or degree

There is a great **disparity** between a light snack and a great feast.

adj.—unconcerned

There he lay, **indifferent** to all the excitement around him.

adj.—touching; adjoining and close, but may not be touching

There are many **contiguous** buildings in the city because there is no excess land to allow space between them.

Questions

ITINERARY

*Your Own Answer*_____

ARID

*Your Own Answer*_____

COLLOQUIAL

*Your Own Answer*_____

Correct Answers

A67

n.—travel plan; schedule; course

Their trip **itinerary** was disrupted by an unexpected snow storm.

A68

adj.—extremely dry; parched; barren; unimaginative

Their thirst became worse due to the **arid** condition of the desert.

A69

adj.—casual; common; conversational; idiomatic

Their **colloquial** manner was not accepted in high society.

Questions

THWART

*Your Own Answer*_____

ZEALOT

*Your Own Answer*_____

NETTLE

*Your Own Answer*_____

Correct Answers

A70

v.—to prevent from accomplishing a purpose; to frustrate

Their attempt to take over the country was **thwarted** by the palace guard.

A71

n.—believer; enthusiast; fan

The **zealot** followed whatever rules the cult leader set.

A72

v.—to annoy; to irritate

The younger brother **nettled** his older sister until she slapped him.

Questions

Q73

RENDER

*Your Own Answer*_____

Q74

RESPITE

*Your Own Answer*_____

Q75

WORKADAY

*Your Own Answer*_____

Correct Answers

A73

v.—to deliver; to provide

The Yorkville First Aid Squad was first on the scene to **render** assistance.

A74

n.—recess; rest period

The workers talked and drank coffee during the **respite**.

A75

adj.—commonplace

The **workaday** meal was not exciting to the world-class chef.

Questions

Q76

WOODEN

*Your Own Answer*_____

Q77

AMASS

*Your Own Answer*_____

Q78

EPITOME

*Your Own Answer*_____

Correct Answers

adj.—to be expressionless or dull

The **wooden** expression of the man made him look like a statue.

v.—to collect together; to accumulate

The women **amassed** a huge collection of price-less diamonds and pearls.

n.—model; typification; representation

The woman chosen to lead the dancers was the **epitome** of true grace.

Questions

Q79

ARCANE

*Your Own Answer*_____

Q80

BEREFT

*Your Own Answer*_____

Q81

PROFUSION

*Your Own Answer*_____

Correct Answers

A79

adj.—obscure; secret; mysterious

The wizard's description of his magic was purposefully **arcane** so that others would be unable to copy it.

A80

adj.—hurt by someone's death

The widower was **bereft** for many years after his wife's death.

A81

n.—great amount; abundance

The wet winter brought about a **profusion** of mosquitoes.

Questions

Q82

BLITHE

*Your Own Answer*_____

_____

Q83

PAVILION

*Your Own Answer*_____

_____

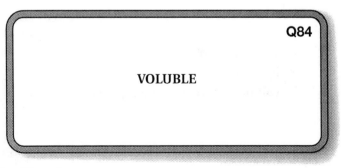

Q84

VOLUBLE

*Your Own Answer*_____

_____

Correct Answers

A82

adj.—happy; cheery; merry
The wedding was a **blithe** celebration.

A83

n.—a large tent or covered area, usually used for entertainment
The wedding **pavilion** was not only beautifully decorated, but also served as welcome protection from a sudden downpour.

A84

adj.—fluent (characterized by a great flow of words, talkative)
The **voluble** host barely let his guests get a word in edgewise.

Questions

Q85

VISCOUS

*Your Own Answer*_____

Q86

STATIC

*Your Own Answer*_____

Q87

SUPERFICIAL

*Your Own Answer*_____

Correct Answers

A85

adj.—thick and sticky (said of fluids)
The **viscous** honey poured slowly from the jar.

A86

adj.—inactive; changeless
The view while riding in the train across the endless, flat landscape remained **static** for days.

A87

adj.—on the surface; narrow minded; lacking depth
The victim had two stab wounds, but luckily they were only **superficial**.

Questions

Q88

IMPERVIOUS

*Your Own Answer*_____

Q89

VERBOSE

*Your Own Answer*_____

Q90

ANTIPATHY

*Your Own Answer*_____

Correct Answers

adj.—impenetrable; not allowing anything to pass through; unaffected

The vest that the policeman wears is **impervious** to bullets.

adj.—wordy; talkative

The **verbose** speech was too long and difficult to follow.

n.—a natural dislike or repugnance

The vegetarian had an **antipathy** toward meat.

Questions

Q91

BIASED

*Your Own Answer*_____

Q92

UPSHOT

*Your Own Answer*_____

Q93

BLASPHEMOUS

*Your Own Answer*_____

Correct Answers

A91

adj.—prejudiced; influenced; not neutral

The vegetarian had a **biased** opinion regarding what should be ordered for dinner.

A92

n.—the final act or result

The **upshot** of the debate was that the bill would be released to the floor.

A93

adj.—irreligious; away from acceptable standards

The upper-class parents thought that it was **blasphemous** for their son to marry a waitress.

Questions

Q94

BELITTLE

*Your Own Answer*_____

Q95

UNRULY

*Your Own Answer*_____

Q96

CONTRAVENE

*Your Own Answer*_____

Correct Answers

A94

v.—to make small; to think lightly of

The unsympathetic friend **belittled** her friend's problems and spoke of her own as the most important.

A95

adj.—not submitting to discipline; disobedient

The **unruly** boys had to be removed from the concert hall.

A96

v.—to act contrary to; to oppose or contradict

The United Nations held that the Eastern European nation had **contravened** the treaty.

Questions

Q97

UNGAINLY

*Your Own Answer*_____

Q98

GUISE

*Your Own Answer*_____

Q99

HEFTY

*Your Own Answer*_____

Correct Answers

adj.—clumsy and unattractive
The **ungainly** man knocked over the plant stand.

n.—appearance
The undercover detective, under the **guise** of friendship, offered to help the drug runner make a connection.

adj.—heavy or powerful
The unabridged dictionary makes for a **hefty** book.

Questions

Q100

IMPLACABLE

Your Own Answer_____

Q101

COLLABORATE

Your Own Answer_____

Q102

TUMID

Your Own Answer_____

Correct Answers

adj.—unwilling to be pacified or appeased

The two-year-old was an **implacable** child; he cried no matter what his parents did to comfort him.

v.—to work together; to cooperate

The two builders **collaborated** to get the house finished.

adj.—swollen; inflated

The **tumid** balloon floated, but the empty one did not.

Questions

Q103

TRUCULENT

*Your Own Answer*_____

Q104

TRANQUILLITY

*Your Own Answer*_____

Q105

TABLE

*Your Own Answer*_____

Correct Answers

A103

adj.—fierce; savage; cruel
The **truculent** beast approached the crowd with
wild eyes and sharpened claws.

A104

n.—peace; stillness; harmony
The **tranquillity** of the tropical island was re-
flected in its calm blue waters and warm sunny
climate.

A105

n.—a systematic list of details
The train schedule was set up as a **table**.

Questions

INFAMY

*Your Own Answer*_____

ABSTRUSE

*Your Own Answer*_____

PETULANT

*Your Own Answer*_____

Correct Answers

A106

n.—a bad reputation

The town had only 98 residents, so all it took was one bad apple to bring **infamy** on the whole place.

A107

adj.—hard to understand; deep; recondite

The topic was so **abstruse**, the student was forced to stop reading.

A108

adj.—peevish; cranky; rude

The tone of his voice and the things that he says become quite **petulant** when he has not gotten enough sleep.

Questions

IMMUTABLE

*Your Own Answer*_____

THRIFTY

*Your Own Answer*_____

AMALGAMATE

*Your Own Answer*_____

Correct Answers

A109

adj.—unchangeable; permanent

The ties that bind alumni to their university are **immutable**.

A110

adj.—economical; penny-wise

The **thrifty** couple saved money by taking the bus to work.

A111

v.—to mix; to merge; to combine

The three presidents decided to **amalgamate** their businesses to build one strong company.

Questions

Q112

SKULK

*Your Own Answer*_____

Q113

DISARRAY

*Your Own Answer*_____

Q114

CANT

*Your Own Answer*_____

Correct Answers

A112

v.—to move secretly, implies sinister intent

The thief **skulked** around the neighborhood hoping to find his next target.

A113

n.—state of disorder

The thief left the house in **disarray**.

A114

n.—insincere or hypocritical statements of high ideals; the jargon of a particular group or occupation

The theater majors had difficulty understanding the **cant** of the computer scientists.

Questions

Q115

VENDETTA

*Your Own Answer*_____

Q116

FORTUITOUS

*Your Own Answer*_____

Q117

VILIFY

*Your Own Answer*_____

Correct Answers

n.—feud

The families' **vendetta** kept them off speaking terms for 50 years.

adj.—happening accidentally

Finding the money under the bush was **fortuitous**.

v.—to speak abusively of

The workers too often **vilify** an employer when upset with working conditions.

Questions

TEPID

*Your Own Answer*_____

COWER

*Your Own Answer*_____

INNOCUOUS

*Your Own Answer*_____

Correct Answers

A118

adj.—lacking warmth, interest, enthusiasm; luke-warm

The **tepid** bath water was perfect for relaxing after a long day.

A119

v.—to crouch down in fear or shame

The tellers **cowered** in the corner as the bandit ransacked the bank.

A120

adj.—harmless; innocent

The teens engaged in an **innocuous** game of touch football.

Questions

Q121

DESECRATE

*Your Own Answer*_____

Q122

KNAVERY

*Your Own Answer*_____

Q123

SARCASM

*Your Own Answer*_____

Correct Answers

A121

v.—to profane; violate the sanctity of

The teenagers' attempt to **desecrate** the church roiled the community.

A122

n.—rascality; trickery

The teacher refused to have **knavery** in his classroom.

A123

n.—ironic; bitter humor designed to wound

The teacher did not appreciate the student's **sarcasm** and gave him detention.

Questions

Q124

CONVOKE

*Your Own Answer*_____

Q125

BREADTH

*Your Own Answer*_____

Q126

SYNTHETIC

*Your Own Answer*_____

Correct Answers

A124

v.—to call to assemble

The teacher **convoked** her students in the auditorium to help prepare them for the play.

A125

n.—the distance from one side to another

The tablecloth was too small to cover the **breadth** of the table.

A126

adj.—not real, rather artificial

The **synthetic** skin was made of a thin rubber.

Questions

Q127

MESMERIZE

*Your Own Answer*_____

Q128

ASEPTIC

*Your Own Answer*_____

Q129

UNDERMINE

*Your Own Answer*_____

Correct Answers

A127

v.—to hypnotize

The swaying motion of the swing **mesmerized** the baby into a deep sleep.

A128

adj.—germ free

The surgeon scrubbed her hands and put on her mask before entering the **aseptic** operating room.

A129

v.—to weaken; to ruin

The supervisor **undermined** the director's power and began controlling the staff.

Questions

VELOCITY

*Your Own Answer*_____

_____

INTERCEDE

*Your Own Answer*_____

_____

CONSTRAIN

*Your Own Answer*_____

_____

Correct Answers

A130

n.—speed

The supersonic transport travels at an amazing **velocity**.

A131

v.—to plead on behalf of another; to mediate

The superpowers were called on to **intercede** in the talks between the two warring nations.

A132

v.—to force, compel; to restrain

The student was **constrained** to remain in her seat until the teacher gave her permission to leave.

Questions

Q133

CHASTISE

*Your Own Answer*_____

Q134

LIAISON

*Your Own Answer*_____

Q135

STRIDENCY

*Your Own Answer*_____

Correct Answers

A133

v.—to punish; to discipline; to admonish; to rebuke

The student was **chastised** for being tardy so frequently.

A134

n.—connection; link

The student council served as a **liaison** between the faculty and the student body.

A135

n.—harshness or shrillness sound

The **stridency** of the whistle hurt the dog's ears.

Questions

Q136

BASTION

*Your Own Answer*_____

Q137

MAR

*Your Own Answer*_____

Q138

SHODDY

*Your Own Answer*_____

Correct Answers

A136

n.—a fortified place or strong defense

The strength of the **bastion** saved the soldiers inside of it.

A137

v.—to damage

The statue was **marred** by the ravages of time.

A138

adj.—of inferior quality; cheap

The state's attorney said many homes, as they were built with **shoddy** materials, were bound to just blow apart even in winds of 60 or 70 miles per hour.

Questions

Q139

STAGNANT

*Your Own Answer*_____

Q140

TENUOUS

*Your Own Answer*_____

Q141

ANECDOTE

*Your Own Answer*_____

Correct Answers

A139

adj.—motionless; uncirculating

The **stagnant** water in the puddle became infested with mosquitoes.

A140

adj.—thin; slim; delicate; weak

The spectators panicked as they watched the cement block dangle from one **tenuous** piece of twine.

A141

n.—a short account of happenings

The speaker told an **anecdote** about how he lost his shoes when he was young.

Questions

DEVOID

*Your Own Answer*_____

CONGLOMERATION

*Your Own Answer*_____

SORDID

*Your Own Answer*_____

Correct Answers

A142

adj.—lacking; empty

The space probe indicated that the planet was **devoid** of any atmosphere.

A143

n.—mixture; collection

The soup was a **conglomeration** of meats and vegetables.

A144

adj.—filthy; base; vile

The **sordid** gutters needed to be cleaned after the long, rainy autumn.

Questions

Q145

SOPORIFIC

*Your Own Answer*_____

_____

Q146

SOLUBILITY

*Your Own Answer*_____

_____

Q147

SOLEMNITY

*Your Own Answer*_____

_____

Correct Answers

A145

adj.—causing sleep

The **soporific** medication should not be taken when you need to drive.

A146

n.—the extent or quality of being soluble; capable of being dissolved

The **solubility** of sugar causes it to disappear when put in water.

A147

n.—seriousness

The **solemnity** of the funeral procession stood in stark contrast to the young children splashing with delight in a nearby pool.

Questions

Q148

STOIC

*Your Own Answer*_____

Q149

FOIST

*Your Own Answer*_____

Q150

WAFT

*Your Own Answer*_____

Correct Answers

A148

adj.—detached; unruffled; calm; austere indifference to joy, grief, pleasure, or pain

The soldier had been in week after week of fierce battle; nonetheless, he remained **stoic**.

A149

v.—to falsely identify as real

The smuggler tried to **foist** the cut glass as a priceless gem.

A150

v.—move gently by wind or breeze

The smoke **wafted** out of the chimney.

Questions

Q151

WHET

*Your Own Answer*_____

Q152

MUNDANE

*Your Own Answer*_____

Q153

SLOTHFUL

*Your Own Answer*_____

Correct Answers

A151

v.—to sharpen
The smell of dinner cooking **whetted** her appetite.

A152

adj.—ordinary; commonplace
The small town was very **mundane**.

A153

adj.—lazy
The **slothful** actions of the player led to his benching.

Questions

Q154

COMPLIANT

*Your Own Answer*_____

Q155

ADEPT

*Your Own Answer*_____

Q156

INAUDIBLE

*Your Own Answer*_____

Correct Answers

A154

adj.—complying; obeying; yielding

The slave was **compliant** with every order to avoid being whipped.

A155

adj.—skilled; practiced

The skilled craftsman was quite **adept** at creating beautiful vases and candleholders.

A156

adj.—not able to be heard

The signals were **inaudible** when the fans began to cheer.

Questions

Q157

RECTIFY

*Your Own Answer*_____

Q158

CORRELATE

*Your Own Answer*_____

Q159

RATIFY

*Your Own Answer*_____

Correct Answers

A157

v.—to correct

The service manager **rectified** the shipping mistake by refunding the customer's money.

A158

v.—to bring into mutual relation

The service man was asked to **correlate** the two computer demonstration pamphlets.

A159

v.—to make valid; confirm

The senate **ratified** the new law that would prohibit companies from discriminating according to race in their hiring practices.

Questions

Q160

SEDITION

*Your Own Answer*_____

Q161

DEBACLE

*Your Own Answer*_____

Q162

STEADFAST

*Your Own Answer*_____

Correct Answers

A160

n.—a revolt

The **sedition** by the guards ended with their being executed for treason.

A161

n.—disaster; collapse; a rout

The Securities and Exchange Commission and the stock exchanges implemented numerous safeguards to head off another **debacle** on Wall Street.

A162

adj.—loyal

The secret service agents are **steadfast** to their oath to protect the president.

Questions

Q163

MALLEABLE

*Your Own Answer*_____

Q164

INDECIPHERABLE

*Your Own Answer*_____

Q165

DISCOURSE

*Your Own Answer*_____

Correct Answers

A163

adj.—easy to shape or bend

The sculptor uses **malleable** substances to create complex masterpieces.

A164

adj.—illegible

The scribbling on the paper is **indecipherable**.

A165

v.—to converse; to communicate in an orderly fashion

The scientists **discoursed** on a conference call for just five minutes but were able to solve three major problems.

Questions

Q166

ARCHETYPE

*Your Own Answer*_____

Q167

AMORPHOUS

*Your Own Answer*_____

Q168

SAGA

*Your Own Answer*_____

Correct Answers

A166

n.—the first model from which others are copied; prototype

The scientist was careful with the **archetype** of her invention so that once manufacturing began, it would be easy to reproduce.

A167

adj.—having no determinate form

The scientist could not determine the sex of the **amorphous** organism.

A168

n.—a legend; any long story of adventure or heroic deed

The **saga** of King Arthur and his court has been told for generations.

Questions

Q169

SOMBER

*Your Own Answer*_____

Q170

SUBJUGATE

*Your Own Answer*_____

Q171

COGITATE

*Your Own Answer*_____

Correct Answers

A169

adj.—dark and depressing; gloomy
The sad story had put everyone in a **somber** mood.

A170

v.—to dominate or enslave

The royal family **subjugated** the peasants, making them perform hard labor.

A171

v.—to think hard; to ponder; to meditate

The room was quiet while every student **cogitated** during the calculus exam.

Questions

Q172

SYMMETRY

*Your Own Answer*_____

Q173

HAMPER

*Your Own Answer*_____

Q174

RETICENT

*Your Own Answer*_____

Correct Answers

A172

n.—correspondence of parts; harmony
The Roman columns give the building a
symmetry.

A173

v.—to interfere with; to hinder
The roadblock **hampered** their progress, but they
knew a shortcut.

A174

adj.—silent; reserved; shy
The **reticent** girl played with her building blocks
while the other children played tag.

Questions

Q175

INCONCLUSIVE

*Your Own Answer*_____

_____

Q176

INCREDULOUS

*Your Own Answer*_____

_____

Q177

REPAST

*Your Own Answer*_____

_____

Correct Answers

A175

adj.—not final or of a definite result

The results being **inconclusive**, the doctors continued to look for a cause of the illness.

A176

adj.—skeptical; unbelieving

The reporter was **incredulous** on hearing the computer executive's UFO account.

A177

n.—food that is eaten

The **repast** consisted of cheese, wine, and bread.

Questions

Q178

PIOUS

*Your Own Answer*_____

Q179

REGAL

*Your Own Answer*_____

Q180

RECALCITRANT

*Your Own Answer*_____

Correct Answers

A178

adj.—religious; devout; dedicated

The religious couple believed that their **pious** method of worship would bring them eternal life.

A179

adj.—royal; grand

The **regal** home was lavishly decorated and furnished with European antiques.

A180

adj.—stubbornly rebellious

The **recalcitrant** youth dyed her hair purple, dropped out of school, and generally worked hard at doing whatever others did not want her to do.

Questions

Q181

REBUFF

*Your Own Answer*_____

Q182

ANTAGONISM

*Your Own Answer*_____

Q183

RAUCOUS

*Your Own Answer*_____

Correct Answers

n.—a blunt refusal to offered help
The **rebuff** of her aid plan came as a shock.

n.—hostility; opposition
The rebellious clan captured a hostage to display **antagonism** to the new peace treaty.

adj.—disagreeable to the sense of hearing; harsh; hoarse
The **raucous** protesters stayed on the street corner all night, shouting their disdain for the whale killers.

Questions

Q184

IMPEDE

*Your Own Answer*_____

Q185

JOCUND

*Your Own Answer*_____

Q186

PULCHRITUDE

*Your Own Answer*_____

Correct Answers

v.—to stop the progress of; to obstruct
The rain **impeded** the work on the building.

adj.—happy; cheerful; genial; gay
The puppy kept a smile on the **jocund** boy's face.

n.—beauty
The **pulchritude** of the girl is seen in her bright smile.

Questions

Q187

PREMISE

*Your Own Answer*_____

Q188

REMORSE

*Your Own Answer*_____

Q189

BENEVOLENT

*Your Own Answer*_____

Correct Answers

A187

n.—the basis for an argument

The prosecutor claimed that the defense lawyer's **premise** was shaky, and thus his whole argument was suspect.

A188

n.—guilt; sorrow

The prosecutor argued that the defendant had shown no **remorse** for his actions.

A189

adj.—kind; generous

The professor proved a tough questioner, but a **benevolent** grader.

Questions

Q190

OBSEQUIOUS

*Your Own Answer*_____

Q191

RUSTIC

*Your Own Answer*_____

Q192

SOVEREIGN

*Your Own Answer*_____

Correct Answers

A190

adj.—servilely attentive; fawning

The princess only seemed to encourage the **obsequious** behavior of her court to enhance her own feeling of superiority.

A191

adj.—plain and unsophisticated; homely; of or living in the country

The couple enjoyed spending weekends at a **rustic** retreat in the woods.

A192

adj.—superior

The power was given to the **sovereign** warrior.

Questions

VERACIOUS

*Your Own Answer*_____

WARRANT

*Your Own Answer*_____

HOMAGE

*Your Own Answer*_____

Correct Answers

A193

adj.—conforming to fact; accurate

The police were certain he had given a **veracious** account because the video confirmed everything.

A194

v.—to justify; to authorize

The police official **warranted** the arrest of the suspect once enough proof had been found.

A195

n.—honor; respect

The police officers paid **homage** to their fallen colleague with a ceremony that celebrated her life.

Questions

POLEMICIST

*Your Own Answer*_____

STANZA

*Your Own Answer*_____

PHLEGMATIC

*Your Own Answer*_____

Correct Answers

A196

n.—a person skilled in argument

The **polemicist** could debate any case skillfully.

A197

n.—group of lines in a poem having a definite pattern

The poet uses an odd simile in the second **stanza** of the poem.

A198

adj.—without emotion or interest

The playwright had hoped his story would take theatergoers on an emotional roller coaster, but on opening night they just sat there, stonefaced and **phlegmatic**.

Questions

Q199

WITHER

*Your Own Answer*_____

Q200

TENSILE

*Your Own Answer*_____

Q201

INDELIBLE

*Your Own Answer*_____

Correct Answers

A199

v.—to wilt; to shrivel; to humiliate; to cut down

The plant **withered** slowly since it received little light and little water.

A200

adj.—undergoing or exerting tension

The pipeline was capable of flexing to withstand the tremendous **tensile** strain that might accompany any seismic movement.

A201

adj.—that which cannot be blotted out or erased

The photograph of Neil Armstrong setting foot on the moon made an **indelible** impression on all who saw it.

Questions

Q202

DEBILITATE

*Your Own Answer*_____

Q203

PERCEPTIVE

*Your Own Answer*_____

Q204

TYRANNY

*Your Own Answer*_____

Correct Answers

A202

v.—to enfeeble; to wear out

The phlebitis **debilitated** him to the point that he was unable even to walk.

A203

adj.—full of insight; aware

The **perceptive** detective discovered that the murder weapon was hidden in a safe under the floor.

A204

n.—absolute power; autocracy

The people were upset because they had no voice in the government that the king ran as a **tyranny**.

Questions

Q205

LACONIC

*Your Own Answer*_____

Q206

PEJORATIVE

*Your Own Answer*_____

Q207

ADVERSARY

*Your Own Answer*_____

Correct Answers

A205

adj.—sparing of words; terse, pithy

The people enjoyed the public addresses of the **laconic** queen.

A206

adj.—making things worse

The **pejorative** comment deepened the dislike between the two families.

A207

n.—an enemy; foe

The peace treaty united two countries that were historically great **adversaries**.

Questions

Q208

DIVERGE

*Your Own Answer*_____

_____

Q209

PARSIMONY

*Your Own Answer*_____

_____

Q210

PARSIMONIOUS

*Your Own Answer*_____

_____

Correct Answers

A208

v.—to separate; to split

The path **diverges** at the old barn, one fork leading to the house, and the other leading to the pond.

A209

n.—a tendency to be over careful in spending

The **parsimony** of the wealthy woman was uncalled for.

A210

adj.—very frugal; unwilling to spend

The **parsimonious** individual argued that twenty-five cents was much too expensive for a pack of gum.

Questions

Q211

INVOKE

*Your Own Answer*_____

Q212

AUGUST

*Your Own Answer*_____

Q213

LUNGE

*Your Own Answer*_____

Correct Answers

v.—to ask for; to call upon

The parishioners **invoked** divine help for their troubles.

adj.—to be imposing or magnificent

The palace was **august** in gold and crystal.

v.—to move suddenly

The owl will **lunge** at its prey in order to take it off guard.

Questions

Q214

INCHOATE

*Your Own Answer*_____

Q215

OBSCURE

*Your Own Answer*_____

Q216

BUNGLER

*Your Own Answer*_____

Correct Answers

A214

adj.—not yet fully formed; rudimentary

The outline of the thesis was the **inchoate** form of a very complex theory.

A215

adj.—not easily understood; dark

The orchestra enjoys performing **obscure** American works, hoping to bring them to a wider audience.

A216

n.—a clumsy person

The one who broke the crystal vase was a true **bungler**.

Questions

Q217

TORPID

*Your Own Answer*_____

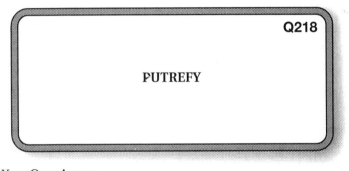

Q218

PUTREFY

*Your Own Answer*_____

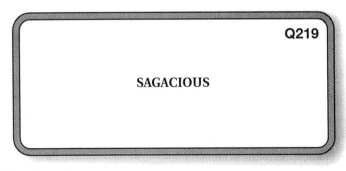

Q219

SAGACIOUS

*Your Own Answer*_____

Correct Answers

adj.—lacking alertness and activity; lethargic
The old, **torpid** dog spent most of his time sleeping.

v.—to decompose; to rot
The old vegetables **putrefied** in the sun.

adj.—wise
The old man gave **sagacious** advice.

Questions

Q220

HALCYON

*Your Own Answer*_____

Q221

FLACCID

*Your Own Answer*_____

Q222

INNUENDO

*Your Own Answer*_____

Correct Answers

A220

adj.—tranquil; happy

The old man fondly remembered his **halcyon** days growing up on the farm.

A221

adj.—lacking firmness

The old dog's **flaccid** tail refused to wag.

A222

n.—hint; insinuation

The office was rife with **innuendo** that a takeover was in the works.

Questions

Q223

REPUDIATE

*Your Own Answer*_____

Q224

OBDURATE

*Your Own Answer*_____

Q225

NOXIOUS

*Your Own Answer*_____

Correct Answers

v.—to reject; to cancel

The offer was **repudiated** because of its cost.

adj.—stubborn

The **obdurate** youngster refused to eat the Brussels sprouts.

adj.—harmful to one's health

The **noxious** fumes caused the person to become ill.

Questions

*Your Own Answer*_____

*Your Own Answer*_____

*Your Own Answer*_____

Correct Answers

A226

n.—a questionable remedy

The **nostrum** of pine leaves and water did not seem to cure the illness.

A227

v.—to make new; to renovate

The Newsomes are **refurbishing** their old colonial home with the help of an interior designer.

A228

n.—a novel or play that uses humor or irony to expose folly

The new play was a **satire** that exposed the president's inability to lead the country.

Questions

Q229

MANDATE

*Your Own Answer*_____

Q230

DETERMINATE

*Your Own Answer*_____

Q231

IMBUE

*Your Own Answer*_____

Correct Answers

n.—order; charge

The new manager wrote a **mandate** declaring that smoking was now prohibited in the office.

adj.—distinct limits

The new laws were very **determinate** as far as what was allowed and what was not allowed.

v.—to dye or to permeate

The new day **imbued** him with a sense of optimism.

Questions

Q232

APPREHENSIVE

*Your Own Answer*_____

Q233

NEFARIOUS

*Your Own Answer*_____

Q234

LETHAL

*Your Own Answer*_____

Correct Answers

adj.—fearful; aware; conscious

The nervous child was **apprehensive** about beginning a new school year.

adj.—villainous or wicked

The **nefarious** ruler killed all the cattle and hoarded all of the food.

adj.—deadly

The natural gas leak caused a **lethal** explosion that killed thousands of innocent people.

Questions

Q235

TACIT

*Your Own Answer*_____

Q236

MALEDICTION

*Your Own Answer*_____

Q237

NARCISSISTIC

*Your Own Answer*_____

Correct Answers

A235

adj.—not voiced or expressed

The National Security Agency aide argued, in effect, that he had received the president's **tacit** approval for the arms-for-hostages deal.

A236

n.—curse; evil spell

The nasty old man shouted **maledictions** at the children.

A237

adj.—egotistical; self-centered; self-love; excessive interest in one's appearance, comfort, abilities, etc.

The **narcissistic** actor was difficult to get along with.

Questions

Q238

KNOTTY

*Your Own Answer*_____

Q239

DEPICT

*Your Own Answer*_____

Q240

MUNIFICENT

*Your Own Answer*_____

Correct Answers

A238

adj.—to be puzzling or hard to explain
The mystery was **knotty**.

A239

v.—to portray; to describe
The mural **depicts** the life of a typical urban dweller.

A240

adj.—very generous in giving; lavish
The **munificent** woman was well liked.

Questions

Q241

DIRGE

*Your Own Answer*_____

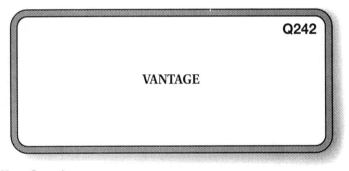

Q242

VANTAGE

*Your Own Answer*_____

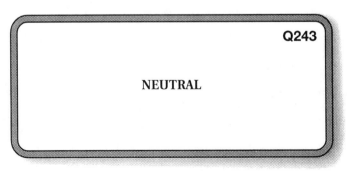

Q243

NEUTRAL

*Your Own Answer*_____

Correct Answers

A241

n.—a hymn for a funeral; a song or poem expressing lament

The mourners sang a traditional Irish **dirge**.

A242

n.—position giving an advantage

The mountaintop was a great **vantage** point for seeing the meteor showers.

A243

adj.—impartial; unbiased

The mother remained **neutral** regarding the argument between her two children.

Questions

Q244

PALLOR

*Your Own Answer*_____

Q245

VENERATE

*Your Own Answer*_____

Q246

MISER

*Your Own Answer*_____

Correct Answers

A244

n.—lack of facial color

The more vivid the testimony grew, the more the witness seemed to take on a ghostly **pallor**.

A245

v.—to revere

The missionary was **venerated** for the help he had given the homeless.

A246

n.—penny-pincher; stingy person

The **miser** made no donations and loved counting his money every night.

Questions

MISANTHROPE

*Your Own Answer*_____

MERCURIAL

*Your Own Answer*_____

MELODIOUS

*Your Own Answer*_____

Correct Answers

A247

n.—a hater of mankind
The **misanthrope** lived alone in the forest.

A248

adj.—quick; changeable; fickle
The **mercurial** actions of the boy kept his parents
unsure of his state of mind.

A249

adj.—pleasing to hear
The **melodious** sounds of the band attracted
many onlookers.

Questions

Q250

ASSUAGE

*Your Own Answer*_____

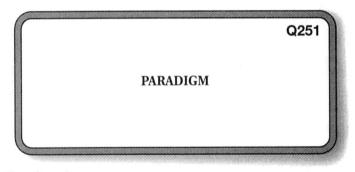

Q251

PARADIGM

*Your Own Answer*_____

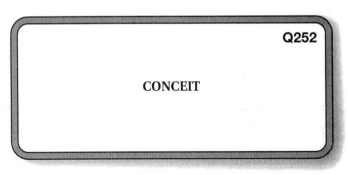

Q252

CONCEIT

*Your Own Answer*_____

Correct Answers

A250

v.— to lessen or calm

The medication helped **assuage** the pain of the wound.

A251

n.—model; prototype; pattern

The Massachusetts gubernatorial race was considered a **paradigm** of campaign civility.

A252

n.—an exaggerated personal opinion

The man's belief that he was the best player on the team was pure **conceit**.

Questions

Q253

APOCRYPHAL

*Your Own Answer*_____

Q254

INGRATIATE

*Your Own Answer*_____

Q255

SCANTY

*Your Own Answer*_____

Correct Answers

adj.—counterfeit; of doubtful authorship or authenticity

The man who said he was a doctor was truly **apocryphal**.

v.—to bring into one's good graces

The man was hoping to **ingratiate** himself with his wife by buying a bouquet of flowers and candy.

adj.—inadequate; sparse

The malnutrition was caused by the **scanty** amount of healthy food eaten each day.

Questions

MALICIOUS

*Your Own Answer*_____

MALEFACTOR

*Your Own Answer*_____

REPROACH

*Your Own Answer*_____

Correct Answers

A256

adj.—spiteful; vindictive

The **malicious** employee slashed her tires for revenge.

A257

n.—an evil person

The **malefactor** ordered everyone to work over the holidays.

A258

v.—to blame and thus make feel ashamed; to rebuke

The major **reproached** his troops for not following orders.

Questions

Q259

LUXURIANT

*Your Own Answer*_____

Q260

BURLY

*Your Own Answer*_____

Q261

CATALYST

*Your Own Answer*_____

Correct Answers

A259

adj.—grown with energy and in great abundance

The **luxuriant** flowers grew in every available space.

A260

adj.—strong; bulky; stocky

The lumberjack was a **burly** man.

A261

n.—anything which creates a situation in which change can occur

The low pressure system was the **catalyst** for the nor'easter.

Questions

Q262

SAUNTER

*Your Own Answer*_____

Q263

CONDONE

*Your Own Answer*_____

Q264

PERCUSSION

*Your Own Answer*_____

Correct Answers

v.—to walk at a leisurely pace; to stroll

The loving couple **sauntered** down the wooded path.

v.—to overlook; to forgive

The loving and forgiving mother **condoned** her son's life of crime.

n.—striking one object against another

The loud **percussion** of the hunter's gunshot startled the birds.

Questions

Q265

CONSTERNATION

*Your Own Answer*_____

_____

Q266

PITTANCE

*Your Own Answer*_____

_____

Q267

COAGULATE

*Your Own Answer*_____

_____

Correct Answers

A265

n.—amazement or terror that causes confusion

The look of **consternation** on the child's face caused her father to panic.

A266

n.—small allowance

The little girl received a **pittance** every week for keeping her room clean.

A267

v.—to become a semisolid, soft mass; to clot

The liquid will **coagulate** and close the tube if left standing.

Questions

Q268

CONUNDRUM

*Your Own Answer*_____

Q269

LECHEROUS

*Your Own Answer*_____

Q270

REBUTTAL

*Your Own Answer*_____

Correct Answers

A268

n.—a puzzle or riddle

The legend says that to enter the secret passageway, one must answer the ancient **conundrum**.

A269

adj.—impure in thought and act

The **lecherous** Humbert Humbert is Nabokov's protagonist in *Lolita*, a novel that sparked great controversy because of Humbert's romantic attachment to a young girl.

A270

n.—refutation

The lawyer's **rebuttal** to the judge's sentencing was to present more evidence to the case.

Questions

Q271

DURESS

*Your Own Answer*_____

Q272

METICULOUS

*Your Own Answer*_____

Q273

IMPALE

*Your Own Answer*_____

Correct Answers

A271

n.—force; constraint

The Labor Department inspector needed to establish whether the plant workers had been held under **duress**.

A272

adj.—exacting; precise

The lab technicians must be **meticulous** in their measurements to obtain exact results.

A273

v.—to pierce through with, or stick on, something pointed

The knight was **impaled** by the sharp lance.

Questions

Q274

REPLETE

*Your Own Answer*_____

Q275

CAPRICE

*Your Own Answer*_____

Q276

SEQUESTER

*Your Own Answer*_____

Correct Answers

A274

adj.—well supplied
The kitchen came **replete** with food and utensils.

A275

n.—a sudden, unpredictable, or whimsical change
The king ruled by **caprice** as much as law.

A276

v.—to separate or segregate
The jury was **sequestered** at the local inn.

Questions

SPECIOUS

*Your Own Answer*_____

APPROBATORY

*Your Own Answer*_____

DESIST

*Your Own Answer*_____

Correct Answers

A277

adj.—plausible, but deceptive; apparently, but not actually true

The jury forewoman said the jury saw through the defense lawyer's **specious** argument and convicted his client on the weight of the evidence.

A278

adj.—approving or sanctioning

The judge showed his acceptance in his **approbatory** remark.

A279

v.—to stop or cease

The judge ordered the man to **desist** from calling his ex-wife in the middle of the night.

Questions

Q280

JOLLITY

*Your Own Answer*_____

Q281

YOKE

*Your Own Answer*_____

Q282

SOLICIT

*Your Own Answer*_____

Correct Answers

A280

n.—being fun or jolly

The crowd's **jollity** was seen in the cheering and laughing.

A281

n.—harness; collar; bond

The jockey led her horse by the **yoke** around its neck and face.

A282

v.—to ask; to seek

The jobless man **solicited** employment from many factories before he was able to find work.

Questions

UNIQUE

*Your Own Answer*_____

JESTER

*Your Own Answer*_____

INVETERATE

*Your Own Answer*_____

Correct Answers

A283

adj.—without equal; incomparable

The jeweler assured him that the dubloon was **unique**, as it was part of the long lost treasure of the Atocha.

A284

n.—a person employed to amuse

The **jester** tried all of his tricks to get the girl to laugh.

A285

adj.—a practice settled on over a long period of time

The **inveterate** induction ceremony bespoke one of the school's great traditions.

Questions

Q286

INTREPID

*Your Own Answer*_____

_____

Q287

CODIFY

*Your Own Answer*_____

_____

Q288

GARBLED

*Your Own Answer*_____

_____

Correct Answers

A286

adj.—fearless; bold

The **intrepid** photographer flew on some of the fiercest bombing raids of the war.

A287

v.—to organize laws or rules into a systematic collection (code)

The intern **codified** all the city's laws into a computerized filing system.

A288

adj.—mixed up; distorted or confused

The interference on the phone line caused the data to become **garbled** on the computer screen.

Questions

Q289

ABASE

*Your Own Answer*_____

Q290

INGENUOUS

*Your Own Answer*_____

Q291

IMPERTURBABLE

*Your Own Answer*_____

Correct Answers

A289

v.—to degrade; to humiliate; to disgrace

The insecure father, after failing to achieve his own lifelong goals, **abased** his children whenever they failed.

A290

adj.—noble; honorable; candid; also naive, simple, artless, without guile

The **ingenuous** doctor had a great bedside manner, especially when it came to laying out the full implications of an illness.

A291

adj.—calm; not easily excited

The **imperturbable** West Point graduate made a fine negotiator.

Questions

SUPPRESS

*Your Own Answer*_____

COMMISERATE

*Your Own Answer*_____

IRREPROACHABLE

*Your Own Answer*_____

Correct Answers

A292

v.—to bring to an end; to hold back

The illegal aliens were **suppressed** by the border patrol.

A293

v.—to show sympathy for

The hurricane victims **commiserated** about the loss of their homes.

A294

adj.—without blame or faults

The honesty of the priest made him **irreproachable**.

Questions

Q295

AFFILIATE

*Your Own Answer*_____

Q296

IRREPARABLE

*Your Own Answer*_____

Q297

HAUGHTY

*Your Own Answer*_____

Correct Answers

A295

v.—to connect or associate with; to accept as a member

The hiking club **affiliated** with the bird-watching club.

A296

adj.—not repairable

The head-on collision left the car **irreparable**.

A297

adj.—to have or show great pride in oneself

The **haughty** girl displayed her work as if she were the most prized artist.

Questions

Q298

ABJECT

*Your Own Answer*_____

Q299

SOJOURN

*Your Own Answer*_____

Q300

CONCEDE

*Your Own Answer*_____

Correct Answers

adj.—of the worst or lowest degree

The Haldemans lived in **abject** poverty, with barely a roof over their heads.

n.—temporary stay; visit

The guest remained only for a **sojourn**; she was going to leave in the afternoon.

v.—1. to acknowledge; to admit 2. to surrender; to abandon one's position

1. After much wrangling, he **conceded** that the minister had a point.
2. Satisfied with the recount, the mayor **conceded** graciously.

Questions

Q301

CONTEMPT

*Your Own Answer*_____

Q302

IMPECUNIOUS

*Your Own Answer*_____

Q303

GRAVITY

*Your Own Answer*_____

Correct Answers

A301

n.—scorn; disrespect

The greedy, selfish banker was often discussed with great **contempt**.

A302

adj.—poor; having no money

The Great Depression made family after family **impecunious**.

A303

n.—seriousness

The **gravity** of the incident was sufficient to involve the police and the FBI.

Questions

Q304

INDICT

*Your Own Answer*_____

Q305

SUPERLATIVE

*Your Own Answer*_____

Q306

GLUTTON

*Your Own Answer*_____

Correct Answers

A304

v.—to charge with a crime

The grand jury **indicted** her and her husband for embezzlement and six other lesser counts.

A305

adj.—of the highest kind or degree

The Golden Gate Bridge is a **superlative** example of civil engineering.

A306

n.—overeater

The **glutton** ate twelve hot dogs.

Questions

Q307

ADAMANT

*Your Own Answer*_____

Q308

BEMUSE

*Your Own Answer*_____

Q309

ORTHODOX

*Your Own Answer*_____

Correct Answers

adj.—not yielding; firm

The girl's parents were **adamant** about not allowing her to go on a dangerous backpacking trip.

v.—to preoccupy in thought

The girl was **bemused** by her troubles.

adj.—traditional; accepted

The gifted child's parents concluded that **orthodox** methods of education would not do their son any good, so they decided to teach him at home.

Questions

EUPHONY

*Your Own Answer*_____

GAUNTLET

*Your Own Answer*_____

URBANE

*Your Own Answer*_____

Correct Answers

A310

n.—pleasant combination of sounds

The gently singing birds created a beautiful **euphony**.

A311

n.—a protective glove

The **gauntlet** saved the man's hand from being burned in the fire.

A312

adj.—cultured; suave

The gala concert and dinner dance was attended by the most **urbane** individuals.

Questions

Q313

MELANCHOLY

*Your Own Answer*_____

Q314

WANE

*Your Own Answer*_____

Q315

DEBASE

*Your Own Answer*_____

Correct Answers

A313

n.—depression; gloom

The funeral parlor was filled with the **melancholy** of mourning.

A314

v.—to grow gradually smaller

The full moon **waned** until it was nothing but a sliver in the sky.

A315

v.—to make lower in quality

The French are concerned that "Franglais," a blending of English and French, will **debase** their language.

Questions

Q316

CHURLISHNESS

*Your Own Answer*_____

Q317

CALAMITY

*Your Own Answer*_____

Q318

VALIANT

*Your Own Answer*_____

Correct Answers

A316

n.—crude or surly behavior; behavior of a peasant

The fraternity's **churlishness** ran afoul of the dean's office.

A317

n.—disaster

The fire in the apartment building was a great **calamity**.

A318

adj.—full of courage or bravery

The firefighter made a **valiant** effort to save the trapped person.

Questions

ACRID

*Your Own Answer*_____

FINITE

*Your Own Answer*_____

INCOGNITO

*Your Own Answer*_____

Correct Answers

A319

adj.—sharp; bitter; foul-smelling

The fire at the plastics factory caused an **acrid** odor to be emitted throughout the surrounding neighborhood.

A320

adj.—measurable; limited; not everlasting

The **finite** amount of stored food will soon run out.

A321

adj.—unidentified; disguised; concealed

The federal Witness Protection Program makes its charges permanently **incognito**.

Questions

Q322

FATUOUS

*Your Own Answer*_____

_____

Q323

ALLOCATE

*Your Own Answer*_____

_____

Q324

ARDENT

*Your Own Answer*_____

_____

Correct Answers

A322

adj.—lacking in seriousness

The **fatuous** prank was meant to add comedy to the situation.

A323

v.—to set aside; to designate; to assign

The farmer **allocated** three acres of his fields to corn.

A324

adj.—with passionate or intense feelings

The fans' **ardent** love of the game kept them returning to watch the terrible team.

Questions

INDIGENCE

*Your Own Answer*_____

SALVAGE

*Your Own Answer*_____

HYPERBOLE

*Your Own Answer*_____

Correct Answers

A325

n.—the condition of being poor

The family's **indigence** was evident by the run-down house they lived in.

A326

v.—to rescue from loss

The family tried to **salvage** their belongings after their home was destroyed by a tornado.

A327

n.—an exaggeration, not to be taken seriously

"The full moon was almost blinding in its brightness," he said with a measure of **hyperbole**.

Questions

Q328

REPLICA

*Your Own Answer*_____

_____

Q329

DEPRECATE

*Your Own Answer*_____

_____

Q330

PRODIGIOUS

*Your Own Answer*_____

_____

Correct Answers

A328

n.—copy; representation; reproduction
The equine sculpture was a **replica** of a Remington.

A329

v.—to express disapproval of; to protest against
The environmentalists **deprecated** the paper companies for cutting down ancient forests.

A330

adj.—exceptional; tremendous
The Empire State Building required a **prodigious** amount of steel to erect.

Questions

Q331

RESILIENT

*Your Own Answer*_____

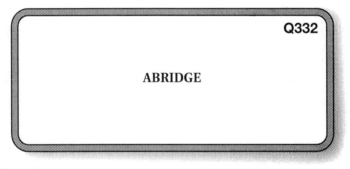

Q332

ABRIDGE

*Your Own Answer*_____

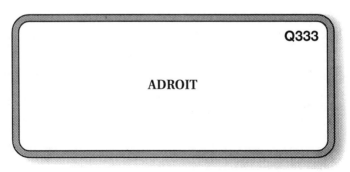

Q333

ADROIT

*Your Own Answer*_____

Correct Answers

A331

adj.—flexible; capable of withstanding stress

The elderly man attributed his **resilient** health to a good diet and frequent exercise.

A332

v.—to shorten; to limit

The editor **abridged** the story to make the book easier to digest.

A333

adj.—clever or expert

The driver's **adroit** driving avoided a serious accident.

Questions

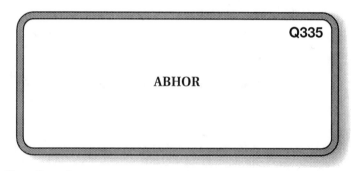

Q334

DOGMA

*Your Own Answer*_____

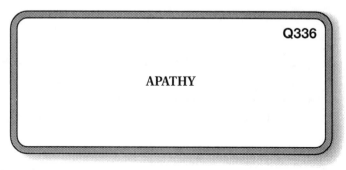

Q335

ABHOR

*Your Own Answer*_____

Q336

APATHY

*Your Own Answer*_____

Correct Answers

A334

n.—a collection of beliefs

The **dogma** of the village was based on superstition.

A335

v.—to hate

The dog **abhorred** cats, chasing and growling at them whenever it had the opportunity.

A336

n.—lack of emotion or interest

The disheartened peasants expressed **apathy** toward the new law which promised new hope and prosperity for all.

Questions

DIN

*Your Own Answer*_____

CONSPICUOUS

*Your Own Answer*_____

OUST

*Your Own Answer*_____

Correct Answers

A337

n.—a noise which is loud and continuous

The **din** of the jackhammers reverberated throughout the concrete canyon.

A338

adj.—easy to see; noticeable

The diligent and hardworking editor thought the mistake was **conspicuous**.

A339

v.—to drive out; to eject

The dictator was **ousted** in a coup d'état.

Questions

Q340

DICHOTOMY

*Your Own Answer*_____

Q341

TANTALIZE

*Your Own Answer*_____

Q342

DEMISE

*Your Own Answer*_____

Correct Answers

n.—a division into two parts or kinds

The **dichotomy** within the party threatens to split it.

v.—to tempt; to torment

The desserts were **tantalizing**, but he was on a diet.

n.—ceasing to exist as in death

The **demise** of Gimbels followed years of decline.

Questions

IMPUGN

*Your Own Answer*_____

_____

INCIDENTAL

*Your Own Answer*_____

_____

ARBITER

*Your Own Answer*_____

_____

Correct Answers

A343

v.—to attack with words; to question one's truth-
fulness or integrity

The defense lawyer **impugned** the witness's testimony, which set back the prosecution's case.

A344

adj.—extraneous; unexpected

The defense lawyer argued that the whereabouts
of the defendant's sneakers were only **incidental**
to the commission of the crime.

A345

n.—one who is authorized to judge or decide

The decision of who would represent the people
was made by the **arbiter**.

Questions

LIMBER

*Your Own Answer*_____

CYNIC

*Your Own Answer*_____

FERVOR

*Your Own Answer*_____

Correct Answers

A346

adj.—flexible; pliant

The dancers must be **limber** to do their ballet steps.

A347

n.—one who believes that others are motivated entirely by selfishness.

The **cynic** felt that the hero saved the man to become famous.

A348

n.—passion; intensity of feeling

The crowd was full of **fervor** as the candidate entered the hall.

Questions

ORNATE

*Your Own Answer*_____

_____

FLEDGLING

*Your Own Answer*_____

_____

DIVERSE

*Your Own Answer*_____

_____

Correct Answers

A349

adj.—elaborate; lavish; decorated
The courthouse was framed by **ornate** friezes.

A350

adj.—inexperienced person; beginner
The course was not recommended for **fledgling** skiers.

A351

adj.—different; varied
The course offerings were so **diverse** I had a tough time choosing.

Questions

Q352

CORPULENCE

*Your Own Answer*_____

_____

Q353

CONNOTATIVE

*Your Own Answer*_____

_____

Q354

REVERENT

*Your Own Answer*_____

_____

Correct Answers

A352

n.—obesity

The **corpulence** of the man kept him from fitting into the seat.

A353

adj.—containing associated meanings in addition to the primary one

The **connotative** meaning of their music was spelled out in the video.

A354

adj.—respectful; feeling or showing deep love, respect, or awe

The congregation was very **reverent** of its spiritual leader.

Questions

Q355

CONCISE

*Your Own Answer*_____

Q356

COMPLAISANCE

*Your Own Answer*_____

Q357

COMMUNAL

*Your Own Answer*_____

Correct Answers

A355

adj.—in few words; brief; condensed

The **concise** instructions were printed on two pages rather than the customary five.

A356

n.—the quality of being agreeable or eager to please

The **complaisance** of the new assistant made it easy for the managers to give him a lot of work without worrying that he may complain.

A357

adj.—shared or common ownership

The **communal** nature of the project made everyone pitch in to help.

Questions

Q358

TRITE

*Your Own Answer*_____

Q359

MIMICRY

*Your Own Answer*_____

Q360

COHESION

*Your Own Answer*_____

Correct Answers

adj.—commonplace; overused

The committee was looking for something new, not the same **trite** ideas.

n.—imitation

The comedian's **mimicry** of the president's gestures had the audience rolling in the aisles.

n.—the act of holding together

The **cohesion** of different molecules forms different substances.

Questions

Q361

COFFER

*Your Own Answer*_____

Q362

NAUTICAL

*Your Own Answer*_____

Q363

SUNDER

*Your Own Answer*_____

Correct Answers

A361

n.—a chest where money or valuables are kept

The **coffer** that contained the jewels was stolen.

A362

adj.—of the sea; having to do with sailors, ships, or navigation

The coastal New England town had a charming **nautical** influence.

A363

v.—to break; to split in two

The Civil War threatened to **sunder** the United States.

Questions

Q364

DISCRETE

*Your Own Answer*_____

Q365

CHORTLE

*Your Own Answer*_____

Q366

CENSOR

*Your Own Answer*_____

Correct Answers

A364

adj.—separate; individually distinct; composed of distinct parts

The citizens' committee maintained that road widening and drainage were hardly **discrete** issues.

A365

v.—to make a gleeful, chuckling sound

The audience **chortled**, indicating it wouldn't be as tough a crowd as the stand-up comic had expected.

A366

v.—to examine and delete objectionable material

The children were allowed to watch the adult movie only after it had been **censored**.

Questions

FLUENCY

*Your Own Answer*_____

BERATE

*Your Own Answer*_____

CIRCUMLOCUTION

*Your Own Answer*_____

Correct Answers

n.—ability to write easily and expressively

The child's **fluency** in Spanish and English was remarkable.

v.—to scold; to reprove; to reproach; to criticize

The child was **berated** by her parents for breaking the china.

n.—a roundabout or indirect way of speaking; not to the point

The child made a long speech using **circumlocution** to avoid stating that it was she who had knocked over the lamp.

Questions

ATTENUATE

*Your Own Answer*_____

UNWONTED

*Your Own Answer*_____

HARMONIOUS

*Your Own Answer*_____

Correct Answers

v.—to make thin or slender; to weaken or dilute

The chemist **attenuated** the solution by adding water.

adj.—not ordinary; unusual

The changed migratory habits of the Canada geese, though **unwonted**, are undesired because of the mess they make.

adj.—having proportionate and orderly parts

The challenge for the new conductor was to mold his musicians' talents into a **harmonious** orchestra.

Questions

COMPLACENT

*Your Own Answer*_____

DEFAMATION

*Your Own Answer*_____

MIRE

*Your Own Answer*_____

Correct Answers

adj.—content; self-satisfied; smug

The CEO worries regularly that his firm's winning ways will make it **complacent**.

n.—to harm a name or reputation; to slander

The carpenter felt that the notoriousness of his former partner brought **defamation** to his construction business.

v.—to cause to get stuck in wet, soggy ground

The car became **mired** in the mud.

Questions

Q376

CAPRICIOUS

*Your Own Answer*_____

_____

Q377

JEOPARDY

*Your Own Answer*_____

_____

Q378

ALOOF

*Your Own Answer*_____

_____

Correct Answers

A376

adj.—changeable; fickle

The **capricious** bride-to-be has a different church in mind for her wedding every few days.

A377

n.—danger; peril

The campers realized they were in potential **jeopardy** when the bears surrounded their camp.

A378

adj.—distant in interest; reserved; cool

The calm defendant remained **aloof** when he was wrongly accused of fabricating his story.

Questions

Q379

CACOPHONOUS

*Your Own Answer*_____

Q380

TYCOON

*Your Own Answer*_____

Q381

PENITENT

*Your Own Answer*_____

Correct Answers

adj.—sounding jarring
The **cacophonous** sound from the bending metal sent shivers up our spines.

n.—wealthy leader
The business **tycoon** prepared to buy his fifteenth company.

adj.—feeling sorry for what one has done
The burglar expressed his **penitent** feelings during his confession.

Questions

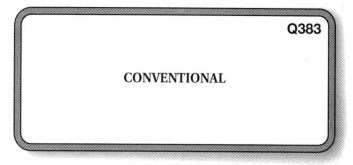

Q382

DISTENTION

*Your Own Answer*_____

Q383

CONVENTIONAL

*Your Own Answer*_____

Q384

CHERISH

*Your Own Answer*_____

Correct Answers

A382

n.—inflation or extension

The bulge in the carpet was caused by the **distention** of the wood underneath.

A383

adj.—traditional; common; routine

The bride wanted a **conventional** wedding ceremony, complete with a white wedding gown, a large bridal party, and a grand reception.

A384

v.—to feel love for

The bride vowed to **cherish** the groom for life.

Questions

Q385

INSUBORDINATE

*Your Own Answer*_____

Q386

INANIMATE

*Your Own Answer*_____

Q387

DIATRIBE

*Your Own Answer*_____

Correct Answers

A385

adj.—disobedient to authority

The boy's **insubordinate** behavior was a constant source of tension between the school and his parents.

A386

adj.—to be dull or spiritless; not animated; not endowed with life

The boy nagged his father for a real puppy, not some **inanimate** stuffed animal.

A387

n.—an abusive criticism

The boss's **diatribe** had everyone scrambling to do a better job.

Questions

BOMBASTIC

*Your Own Answer*_____

PROMONTORY

*Your Own Answer*_____

CEREMONIOUS

*Your Own Answer*_____

Correct Answers

A388

adj.—pompous; wordy; turgid
The **bombastic** woman talks a lot about herself.

A389

n.—a piece of land jutting into a body of water
The boat hit the rocky **promontory**, splitting the bow.

A390

adj.—very formal or proper
The black-tie dinner was highly **ceremonious**.

Questions

Q391

AVIARY

*Your Own Answer*_____

Q392

RETROACTION

*Your Own Answer*_____

Q393

QUIESCENT

*Your Own Answer*_____

Correct Answers

A391

n.—a large place to keep birds

The birds were being stored in the **aviary**.

A392

n.—effect, as of a law, of things done prior to the enactment

The bill's **retroaction** stood to save taxpayers an average of $500 a head.

A393

adj.—inactive; at rest

The Bible says that the Lord created the Earth in six days, and, on the seventh, He was **quiescent**.

Questions

CACOPHONY

*Your Own Answer*_____

INTRANSIGENT

*Your Own Answer*_____

BAROQUE

*Your Own Answer*_____

Correct Answers

A394

n.—a harsh, inharmonious collection of sounds; dissonance

The beautiful harmony of the symphony was well enjoyed after the **cacophony** coming from the stage as the orchestra warmed up.

A395

adj.—uncompromising

The baseball owners and players remained **intransigent**, so a deal was never struck.

A396

adj.—extravagant; ornate

The **baroque** artwork was made up of intricate details, which kept the museum-goers enthralled.

Questions

FEALTY

*Your Own Answer*_____

ACCOMPLICE

*Your Own Answer*_____

AZURE

*Your Own Answer*_____

Correct Answers

A397

n.—loyalty
The baron was given land in exchange for his **fealty** to the king.

A398

n.—co-conspirator; partner; partner-in-crime
The bank robber's **accomplice** drove the getaway car.

A399

adj.—the clear blue color of the sky
The **azure** sky made the picnic day perfect.

Questions

AVARICE

*Your Own Answer*_____

AUTOCRAT

*Your Own Answer*_____

JUXTAPOSE

*Your Own Answer*_____

Correct Answers

A400

n.—a greed for wealth

The **avarice** of the president led to his downfall.

A401

n.—an absolute ruler

The **autocrat** made every decision and divided the tasks among his subordinates.

A402

v.—to place side-by-side

The author decided to **juxtapose** the two sentences since each one strengthened the meaning of the other.

Questions

Q403

AUSTERE

*Your Own Answer*_____

Q404

CODA

*Your Own Answer*_____

Q405

AUDACIOUS

*Your Own Answer*_____

Correct Answers

adj.—harsh; severe; strict; very plain, lacking ornament

The **austere** teacher assigned five pages of homework each day.

n.—in music, a concluding passage

The audience knew that the concerto was about to end when they heard the orchestra begin playing the **coda**.

adj.—fearless; bold

The **audacious** soldier went into battle without a shield.

Questions

Q406

ATYPICAL

*Your Own Answer*_____

_____

Q407

CONCILIATION

*Your Own Answer*_____

_____

Q408

ASTUTE

*Your Own Answer*_____

_____

Correct Answers

A406

adj.—something that is abnormal

The **atypical** behavior of the wild animal alarmed the hunters.

A407

n.—an attempt to make friendly or placate

The attempt at **conciliation** between the two enemies was futile.

A408

adj.—cunning; sly; crafty

The **astute** lawyer's questioning convinced the jury of the defendant's guilt.

Questions

Q409

ASPIRANT

*Your Own Answer*_____

Q410

ASPERITY

*Your Own Answer*_____

Q411

CONDESCEND

*Your Own Answer*_____

Correct Answers

A409

n.—a person who goes after high goals

The **aspirant** would not settle for assistant director—only the top job was good enough.

A410

n.—harshness

The **asperity** of the winter had almost everybody yearning for spring.

A411

v.—to come down from one's position or dignity

The arrogant, rich man was usually **condescending** toward his servants.

Questions

Q412

AROMATIC

*Your Own Answer*_____

Q413

PUTREFACTION

*Your Own Answer*_____

Q414

ANARCHIST

*Your Own Answer*_____

Correct Answers

A412

adj.—having a smell which is sweet or spicy

The **aromatic** smell coming from the oven made the man's mouth water.

A413

n.—a smelly mass that is the decomposition of organic matter

The apple was nothing but a **putrefaction** after sitting on the windowsill for three weeks.

A414

n.—one who believes that a formal government is unnecessary

The **anarchist** attempted to overthrow the established democratic government of the new nation and reinstate chaos and disarray.

Questions

AMITY

*Your Own Answer*_____

AMIABLE

*Your Own Answer*_____

AMENDMENT

*Your Own Answer*_____

Correct Answers

A415

n.—friendly relations

The **amity** between the two bordering nations put the populations at ease.

A416

adj.—friendly

The **amiable** old man often entertained neighbors and friends with his banjo picking.

A417

n.—a positive change

The **amendment** in his ways showed there was still reason for hope.

Questions

AMBIVALENT

*Your Own Answer*_____

AMBIGUOUS

*Your Own Answer*_____

ALTRUISTIC

*Your Own Answer*_____

Correct Answers

adj.—undecided

The **ambivalent** jury could not reach a unanimous verdict.

adj.—not clear; uncertain; vague

The **ambiguous** law did not make a clear distinction between the new and old land boundary.

adj.—unselfish

The **altruistic** volunteer donated much time and energy in an effort to raise funds for the children's hospital.

Questions

Q421

PERJURY

*Your Own Answer*_____

Q422

INCOMPETENCE

*Your Own Answer*_____

Q423

ALCHEMIST

*Your Own Answer*_____

Correct Answers

A421

n.—the practice of lying

The already sensational trial of a star athlete turned all the more so when it turned out that a police detective had committed **perjury**.

A422

n.—failing to meet necessary requirements

The alleged **incompetence** of the construction crew would later become the subject of a class-action suit.

A423

n.—a person who studies chemistry

The **alchemist**'s laboratory was full of bottles and tubes of strange looking liquids.

Questions

Q424

ALLEVIATE

*Your Own Answer*_____

Q425

ADULATION

*Your Own Answer*_____

Q426

ADAGE

*Your Own Answer*_____

Correct Answers

A424

v.—to lessen or make easier

The airport's monorail **alleviates** vehicular traffic.

A425

n.—high praise

The **adulation** given to the movie star was sickening.

A426

n.—an old saying now accepted as being truthful

The **adage** "Do unto others as you wish them to do unto you" has the very ring of logic and good sense.

Questions

Q427

PRODIGAL

*Your Own Answer*_____

Q428

DISAVOW

*Your Own Answer*_____

Q429

ABRUPT

*Your Own Answer*_____

Correct Answers

A427

adj.—wasteful; lavish

The actor's **prodigal** lifestyle ultimately led to his undoing.

A428

v.—to deny; to refuse to acknowledge

The actor has **disavowed** the rumor.

A429

adj.—happening or ending unexpectedly

The **abrupt** end to their marriage was a shock to everyone.

Questions

Q430

STIGMA

*Your Own Answer*_____

Q431

VIRTUOSO

*Your Own Answer*_____

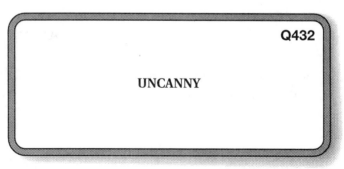

Q432

UNCANNY

*Your Own Answer*_____

Correct Answers

A430

n.—a mark of disgrace
The "F" on his transcript is a **stigma** on his record.

A431

n.—highly skilled artist
The **virtuoso** performed with the best orchestras in the world.

A432

adj.—of a strange nature; weird
That two people could be so alike was **uncanny**.

Questions

Q433

AMALGAM

*Your Own Answer*_____

_____

Q434

LUSTROUS

*Your Own Answer*_____

_____

Q435

RANCOR

*Your Own Answer*_____

_____

Correct Answers

A433

n.—a mixture or combination (often of metals)

That ring is made from an **amalgam** of minerals; if it were pure gold, it would never hold its shape.

A434

adj.—bright; radiant; shining

Surrounded by rubies, the **lustrous** diamond looked magnificent.

A435

n.—strong ill will; enmity

Sure they had their disagreements, but there was no **rancor** between them.

Questions

Q436

OSTENTATIOUS

*Your Own Answer*_____

Q437

NEOLOGISM

*Your Own Answer*_____

Q438

WHIMSICAL

*Your Own Answer*_____

Correct Answers

A436

adj.—being showy

Sure he'd won the lottery, but coming to work in a stretch limo seemed a bit **ostentatious**.

A437

n.—giving a new meaning to an old word

"Bad" is a **neologism** for good.

A438

adj.—fanciful; amusing

Strolling down Disney World's Main Street is bound to put child and adult alike in a **whimsical** mood.

Questions

Q439

MOLTEN

*Your Own Answer*_____

Q440

PERNICIOUS

*Your Own Answer*_____

Q441

SPURIOUS

*Your Own Answer*_____

Correct Answers

A439

adj.—melted

Steel becomes **molten** after heating it to thousands of degrees.

A440

adj.—dangerous; harmful

Standing oil combined with a fresh rain on asphalt can have a **pernicious** impact on a driver's control of the road.

A441

adj.—not genuine; false; bogus

Spurious claims by the importer hid the fact that prison labor had been used in the garments' fabrication.

Questions

Q442

TRANSMUTATION

*Your Own Answer*_____

Q443

RIBALD

*Your Own Answer*_____

Q444

REPREHENSIBLE

*Your Own Answer*_____

Correct Answers

A442

n.—a changed form

Somewhere in the network's entertainment division, the show underwent a **transmutation** from a half-hour sitcom into an hour-long drama.

A443

adj.—vulgar joking or mocking

Some people find the comedian's **ribald** act offensive.

A444

adj.—wicked; disgraceful

Slashing their tires was a **reprehensible** act.

Questions

Q445

SINUOUS

*Your Own Answer*_____

Q446

PRAGMATIC

*Your Own Answer*_____

Q447

INEPT

*Your Own Answer*_____

Correct Answers

adj.—full of curves; twisting and turning

Sinuous mountain roads present extra danger at night when it's harder to see the road's edge.

adj.—matter-of-fact; practical

Since they were saving money to buy a new home, the **pragmatic** married couple decided not to go on an expensive vacation.

adj.—incompetent; clumsy

She would rather update the budget book herself since her assistant is so **inept**.

Questions

QUALIFIED

*Your Own Answer*_____

ULTERIOR

*Your Own Answer*_____

LAX

*Your Own Answer*_____

Correct Answers

A448

adj.—experienced; indefinite

She was well **qualified** for the job after working the field for ten years.

A449

adj.—buried; concealed; undisclosed

She was usually very selfish, so when she came bearing gifts, he suspected that she had **ulterior** motives.

A450

adj.—careless; irresponsible

She was **lax** in everything she did and, therefore, could not be trusted with important tasks.

Questions

Q451

PENSIVE

*Your Own Answer*_____

Q452

LOQUACIOUS

*Your Own Answer*_____

Q453

AUTOCRACY

*Your Own Answer*_____

Correct Answers

A451

adj.—reflective; contemplative

She was in a **pensive** mood, just wanting to be alone to think.

A452

adj.—very talkative; garrulous

She was having difficulty ending the conversation with her **loquacious** neighbor.

A453

n.—an absolute monarchy; government where one person holds power

She was extremely power-hungry and, therefore, wanted her government to be an **autocracy**.

Questions

Q454

DISPASSIONATE

*Your Own Answer*_____

Q455

SUAVE

*Your Own Answer*_____

Q456

JOVIAL

*Your Own Answer*_____

Correct Answers

A454

adj.—lack of feeling; impartial

She was a very emotional person and could not work with such a **dispassionate** employer.

A455

adj.—effortlessly gracious

She was a **suave** negotiator, always getting what she wanted without anyone feeling they'd lost anything.

A456

adj.—cheery; jolly; playful

She was a **jovial** person, always pleasant and fun to be with.

Questions

Q457

WAIVE

*Your Own Answer*_____

Q458

CHAGRIN

*Your Own Answer*_____

Q459

MITIGATE

*Your Own Answer*_____

Correct Answers

A457

v.—to give up possession or right

She wanted to represent herself and, therefore, **waived** her right to an attorney.

A458

n.—distress; shame

She turned red-faced with **chagrin** when she learned that her son had been caught shoplifting.

A459

v.—to alleviate; to lessen; to soothe

She tried to **mitigate** the loss of his pet by buying him a kitten.

Questions

TARRY

*Your Own Answer*_____

SATURATE

*Your Own Answer*_____

STIPEND

*Your Own Answer*_____

Correct Answers

v.—to go or move slowly; to delay

She **tarried** too long and missed her train.

v.—to soak thoroughly; to drench

She **saturated** the sponge with soapy water before she began washing the car.

n.—payment for work done

She receives a monthly **stipend** for her help with the project.

Questions

Q463

VALOR

*Your Own Answer*_____

Q464

NOSTALGIC

*Your Own Answer*_____

Q465

PARAPHERNALIA

*Your Own Answer*_____

Correct Answers

A463

n.—bravery

She received a medal for her **valor** during the war.

A464

adj.—longing for the past; filled with bittersweet memories

She loved her new life, but became **nostalgic** when she met with her old friends.

A465

n.—equipment; accessories

She looked guilty since the drug **paraphernalia** was found in her apartment.

Questions

Q466

INNOVATE

*Your Own Answer*_____

Q467

CHARISMA

*Your Own Answer*_____

Q468

PRISTINE

*Your Own Answer*_____

Correct Answers

v.—to introduce a change; to depart from the old

She **innovated** a new product for the home construction market.

n.—appeal; magnetism; presence

She has such **charisma** that everyone likes her the first time they meet her.

adj.—primitive; pure; uncorrupted

She had such a **pristine** look about her, you would have thought she was an angel.

Questions

Q469

MALEVOLENT

*Your Own Answer*_____

Q470

QUIXOTIC

*Your Own Answer*_____

Q471

GLOAT

*Your Own Answer*_____

Correct Answers

adj.—wishing evil (opposite: benevolent)
She had **malevolent** feelings toward her sister.

adj.—foolishly idealistic
She had a **quixotic** view of the world, believing that humans need never suffer.

v.—brag; to glory over
She **gloated** over the fact that she received the highest score on the exam, annoying her class-mates to no end.

Questions

SUSCEPTIBLE

*Your Own Answer*_____

DUPLICITY

*Your Own Answer*_____

LUCRATIVE

*Your Own Answer*_____

Correct Answers

adj.—easily imposed; inclined

She gets an annual flu shot since she is **susceptible** to becoming ill.

n.—deception

She forgave his **duplicity** but divorced him anyway.

adj.—profitable; gainful

She entered the pharmaceutical industry in the belief that it would be **lucrative**.

Questions

ALTRUISM

*Your Own Answer*_____

DELINEATE

*Your Own Answer*_____

RIGOR

*Your Own Answer*_____

Correct Answers

n.—unselfish devotion to the welfare of others rather than self

She displayed such **altruism** by giving up all of her belongings and joining the Peace Corps in Africa.

v.—to outline; to describe

She **delineated** her plan so that everyone would have a basic understanding of it.

n.—severity

She criticized the planning board's vote with **rigor**.

Questions

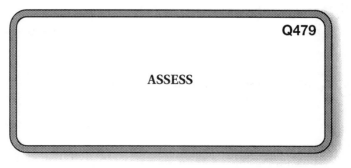

Q478

TERSE

*Your Own Answer*_____

Q479

ASSESS

*Your Own Answer*_____

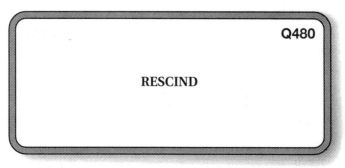

Q480

RESCIND

*Your Own Answer*_____

Correct Answers

A478

adj.—concise; abrupt

She believed in getting to the point, so she always gave **terse** answers.

A479

v.—to estimate the value of

She **assessed** the possible rewards to see if the project was worth her time and effort.

A480

v.—to retract; to discard; to revoke, repeal, or cancel

Sensing that the intent of the regulation had long ago been realized, the city agency **rescinded** the order.

Questions

Q481

FULMINATE

*Your Own Answer*_____

Q482

OMINOUS

*Your Own Answer*_____

Q483

POTABLE

*Your Own Answer*_____

Correct Answers

A481

v.—to issue a strong denunciation

Senator Shay **fulminated** against her opponent's double standard on campaign finance reform.

A482

adj.—threatening

Seeing **ominous** clouds on the horizon, the street fair organizers decided to fold up their tent and go home.

A483

n.—a beverage that is drinkable

Sea water isn't **potable**.

Questions

Q484

VAGABOND

*Your Own Answer*_____

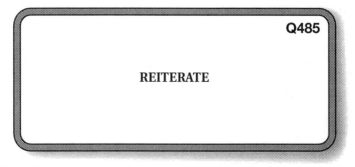

Q485

REITERATE

*Your Own Answer*_____

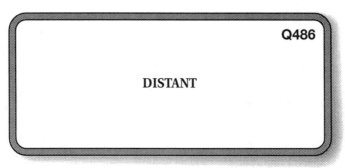

Q486

DISTANT

*Your Own Answer*_____

Correct Answers

n.—wanderer; one without a fixed place

Sam was the kind of **vagabond** who enjoyed hitching a ride on a freight train just to see where it would take him.

v.—to repeat

Rose found that she had to **reiterate** almost everything, leading her to fear her husband was going deaf.

adj.—having separations or being reserved

Rolonda's friends have become more **distant** in recent years.

Questions

Q487

CHOLERIC

*Your Own Answer*_____

Q488

SYCOPHANT

*Your Own Answer*_____

Q489

ARBITRARY

*Your Own Answer*_____

Correct Answers

A487

adj.—cranky; cantankerous; easily angered

Rolly becomes **choleric** when his views are challenged.

A488

n.—flatterer

Rodolfo honed his skills as a **sycophant**, hoping it would get him into Sylvia's good graces.

A489

adj.—based on one's preference or judgment

Rick admitted his decision had been **arbitrary**, as he claimed no expertise in the matter.

Questions

OCCULT

*Your Own Answer*_____

CONTRITE

*Your Own Answer*_____

VIRULENT

*Your Own Answer*_____

Correct Answers

adj.—mystical; mysterious

Relating to the **occult** world means entering a new realm.

adj.—regretful; sorrowful

Regretting his decision not to attend college, the **contrite** man did not lead a very happy life.

adj.—deadly; harmful; malicious

Rattlesnakes use a **virulent** substance to kill their prey.

Questions

ABOMINATE

*Your Own Answer*_____

FACILITATE

*Your Own Answer*_____

PREVALENT

*Your Own Answer*_____

Correct Answers

A493

v.—to loathe; to hate

Randall **abominated** all the traffic he encountered on every morning commute.

A494

v.—to make easier; to simplify

Ramps **facilitate** the entrance to buildings for many people.

A495

adj.—generally occurring

Rain is usually more **prevalent** than snow during April.

Questions

PEDANTIC

*Your Own Answer*_____

UNIVERSAL

*Your Own Answer*_____

OBLITERATE

*Your Own Answer*_____

Correct Answers

A496

adj.—emphasizing minutiae or form in scholarship or teaching

Professor Jones's lectures were so **pedantic** that his students sometimes had a tough time understanding the big picture.

A497

adj.—concerning everyone; existing everywhere

Pollution does not affect just one country or state—it's a **universal** problem.

A498

v.—destroy completely

Poaching nearly **obliterated** the world's whale population.

Questions

Q499

INDIGENOUS

*Your Own Answer*_____

Q500

PERPETUAL

*Your Own Answer*_____

Q501

CHIMERA

*Your Own Answer*_____

Correct Answers

A499

adj.—native to a region; inborn or innate
Piranha are **indigenous** to the tropics.

A500

adj.—never ceasing; continuous
Perpetual pain keeps the woman from walking.

A501

n.—an impossible fancy
Perhaps he saw a flying saucer, but perhaps it was only a **chimera**.

Questions

Q502

CANDID

*Your Own Answer*_____

Q503

EXORBITANT

*Your Own Answer*_____

Q504

UNIFORM

*Your Own Answer*_____

Correct Answers

adj.—honest; truthful; sincere
People trust her because she's so **candid**.

adj.—going beyond what is reasonable; excessive
Paying hundreds of dollars for the dress is an **exorbitant** amount.

adj.—consistent; unvaried; unchanging
Patrons of fast-food chains say they like the idea of a **uniform** menu wherever they go.

Questions

OSSIFY

*Your Own Answer*_____

SLANDER

Q506

*Your Own Answer*_____

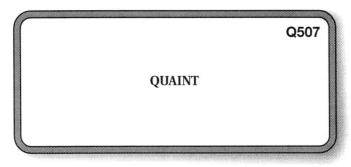

QUAINT

Q507

*Your Own Answer*_____

Correct Answers

A505

v.—to turn to bone; to harden

Over time, the plant matter has **ossified**.

A506

v.—to defame; to maliciously misrepresent

Orville said he'd been **slandered**, and he asked the court who would—or could—give him his name back.

A507

adj.—old-fashioned; unusual; odd

One of the attractions of the bed-and-breakfast is its **quaint** setting in a charming New England village.

Questions

DESTITUTE

*Your Own Answer*_____

RETRACT

*Your Own Answer*_____

COGNITIVE

*Your Own Answer*_____

Correct Answers

A508

adj.—poor; poverty-stricken

One Bangladeshi bank makes loans to **destitute** citizens so that they may overcome their poverty.

A509

v.—to draw or take back

Once you say something, it's hard to **retract**.

A510

adj.—possessing the power to think or meditate; meditative; capable of perception

Once the toddler was able to solve puzzles, it was obvious that her **cognitive** abilities were developing.

Questions

Q511

BREVITY

*Your Own Answer*_____

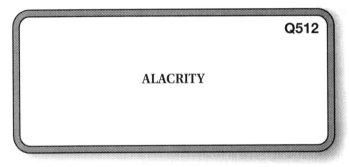

Q512

ALACRITY

*Your Own Answer*_____

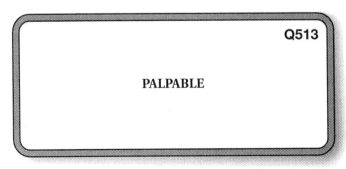

Q513

PALPABLE

*Your Own Answer*_____

Correct Answers

A511

n.—briefness; shortness

On Top 40 AM radio, **brevity** was the coin of the realm.

A512

n.—cheerful promptness or speed

On the first day of her new job, the recent college graduate was able to leave early after completing all of her tasks with **alacrity**.

A513

adj.—touchable; clear; obvious

On a flight that had included a sudden 5,000-foot drop, the passengers' relief upon landing was **palpable**.

Questions

ANONYMOUS

*Your Own Answer*_____

BANEFUL

*Your Own Answer*_____

TENTATIVE

*Your Own Answer*_____

Correct Answers

A514

adj.—nameless; unidentified

Not wishing to be identified by the police, he remained **anonymous** by returning the money he had stolen by sending it through the mail.

A515

adj.—deadly or causing distress, death

Not wearing a seat belt could be **baneful**.

A516

adj.—not confirmed; indefinite

Not knowing if he'd be able to get the days off, Al went ahead anyway and made **tentative** vacation plans with his pal.

Questions

Q517

OPAQUE

*Your Own Answer*_____

Q518

GARRULOUS

*Your Own Answer*_____

Q519

DERIDE

*Your Own Answer*_____

Correct Answers

A517

adj.—dull; cloudy; non-transparent

Not having been washed for years, the once beautiful windows of the Victorian home became **opaque**.

A518

adj.—extremely talkative or wordy

No one wanted to speak with the **garrulous** man for fear of being stuck in a long, one-sided conversation.

A519

v.—to laugh at with contempt; to mock

No matter what he said, he was **derided**.

Questions

Q520

ICONOCLAST

*Your Own Answer*_____

_____

Q521

NEGLIGENCE

*Your Own Answer*_____

_____

Q522

FOIBLE

*Your Own Answer*_____

_____

Correct Answers

n.—one who smashes revered images; an attacker of cherished beliefs

Nietzche's attacks on government, religion, and custom made him an **iconoclast** of grand dimension.

n.—carelessness

Negligence contributed to the accident: she was traveling too fast for the icy conditions.

n.—a minor weakness of character

My major **foible** is an inability to resist chocolate.

Questions

Correct Answers

A523

n.—musical discord; a mingling of inharmonious sounds; nonmusical; disagreement; lack of harmony

Much twentieth-century music is not liked by classical music lovers because of the **dissonance** it holds and the harmonies it lacks.

A524

adj.—two-faced; deceptive

Most of his constituents believed the governor was **hypocritical** for calling his opponent a "mud-slinging hack" when his own campaign had slung more than its share of dirt.

A525

adj.—polytheistic

Moses, distraught over some of his people's continuing **pagan** ways, smashed the stone tablets bearing the Ten Commandments.

Questions

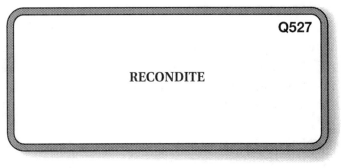

Q526

LOITER

*Your Own Answer*_____

Q527

RECONDITE

*Your Own Answer*_____

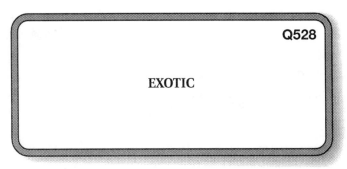

Q528

EXOTIC

*Your Own Answer*_____

Correct Answers

v.—to spend time aimlessly

Many teenagers **loiter** around the mall when there is nothing else to do.

adj.—hard to understand; concealed; characterized by profound scholarship

Many scientific theories are **recondite**, and therefore not known at all by the general public.

adj.—unusual; striking; foreign

Many people asked the name of her **exotic** perfume.

Questions

DUBIOUS

*Your Own Answer*_____

LIVID

*Your Own Answer*_____

INTERMITTENT

*Your Own Answer*_____

Correct Answers

A529

adj.—doubtful; uncertain; skeptical; suspicious

Many people are **dubious** about the possibility of intelligent life on other planets.

A530

adj.—1. black-and-blue; discolored 2. enraged; irate

1. After the accident, her leg was **livid**.
2. When she found out she had been robbed, the woman was **livid**.

A531

adj.—periodic; occasional

Luckily, the snow was only **intermittent**, so the accumulation was slight.

Questions

Q532

USURY

*Your Own Answer*_____

Q533

KINSHIP

*Your Own Answer*_____

Q534

MENAGERIE

*Your Own Answer*_____

Correct Answers

A532

n.—the art of lending money at illegal rates of interest

Loan sharks frequently practice **usury**, but their debtors usually have little choice but to keep quiet and pay up.

A533

n.—family relationship; affinity

Living in close proximity increased the **kinship** of the family.

A534

n.—a place to keep or a collection of wild or strange animals

Little Ryan couldn't wait to visit the zoo to see the **menagerie** of wild boars.

Questions

Q535

LEVITY

*Your Own Answer*_____

Q536

RANCID

*Your Own Answer*_____

Q537

LASSITUDE

*Your Own Answer*_____

Correct Answers

A535

n.—silliness; lack of seriousness
Levity is a necessary trait for a comedian.

A536

adj.—having a bad odor
Left out too long, the meat turned **rancid**.

A537

n.—a state of being tired or listless
Lassitude was evident in the nurses who had been working for 24 hours straight.

Questions

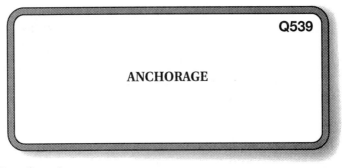

Q538

COMPROMISE

*Your Own Answer*_____

Q539

ANCHORAGE

*Your Own Answer*_____

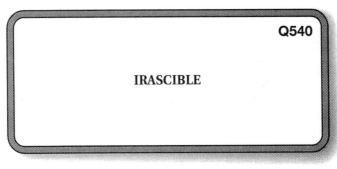

Q540

IRASCIBLE

*Your Own Answer*_____

Correct Answers

A538

v.—to settle by mutual adjustment

Labor leaders and the automakers **compromised** by agreeing to a starting wage of $16 an hour in exchange for concessions on health-care premiums.

A539

n.—something that can be relied on

Knowing the neighbors were right next door was an **anchorage** for the elderly woman.

A540

adj.—prone to anger

Knowing that the king was **irascible**, the servants decided not to tell him about the broken crystal.

Questions

Q541

PROVERBIAL

*Your Own Answer*_____

_____

Q542

HACKNEYED

*Your Own Answer*_____

_____

Q543

HAGGARD

*Your Own Answer*_____

_____

Correct Answers

A541

adj.—well-known because it is commonly referred to

King Solomon's **proverbial** wisdom has been admired through the ages.

A542

adj.—commonplace; trite

Just when you thought neckties were becoming a **hackneyed** gift item, along comes the Grateful Dead collection.

A543

adj.—tired-looking; fatigued

Just by looking at her **haggard** features, you can tell she has not slept for many hours.

Questions

Q544

COMPREHENSIVE

*Your Own Answer*_____

_____

Q545

TOXIC

*Your Own Answer*_____

_____

Q546

IRRATIONAL

*Your Own Answer*_____

_____

Correct Answers

A544

adj.—all-inclusive; complete; thorough

It's the only health facility around to offer **comprehensive** care.

A545

adj.—poisonous

It's best to store cleansing solutions out of children's reach because of their **toxic** contents.

A546

adj.—not logical

It would be **irrational** to climb Mt. Everest without some very warm clothing.

Questions

BEHOOVE

*Your Own Answer*_____

PROFOUND

*Your Own Answer*_____

INSTIGATE

*Your Own Answer*_____

Correct Answers

A547

v.—to be advantageous; to be necessary

It will **behoove** the students to buy their textbooks early.

A548

adj.—deep; knowledgeable; thorough

It was with **profound** regret and sorrow that the family had to leave their homeland for a more prosperous country.

A549

v.—to start; to provoke

It was uncertain to the police as to which party **instigated** the riot.

Questions

CONVERGE

*Your Own Answer*_____

IGNOBLE

*Your Own Answer*_____

CHARLATAN

*Your Own Answer*_____

Correct Answers

v.—to move toward one point (opposite: diverge)

It was obvious that an accident was going to occur as the onlookers watched the two cars **converge**.

adj.—shameful; dishonorable

It was **ignoble** to disgrace the family in front of all of the townspeople.

n.—an impostor; fake

It was finally discovered that the **charlatan** sitting on the throne was not the real king.

Questions

UNOBTRUSIVE

*Your Own Answer*_____

VACILLATION

*Your Own Answer*_____

COGNIZANT

*Your Own Answer*_____

Correct Answers

adj.—inconspicuous; reserved

It was easy to miss the **unobtrusive** plaque above the fireplace.

n.—fluctuation

It was difficult to draw a conclusion from the experiments since there was so much **vacillation** in the results.

adj.—aware of; perceptive

It was critical to establish whether the defendant was **cognizant** of his rights.

Questions

INADVERTENT

*Your Own Answer*_____

VOLATILE

*Your Own Answer*_____

TRAUMATIC

*Your Own Answer*_____

Correct Answers

adj.—not on purpose; unintentional

It was an **inadvertent** error, to be sure, but none-theless a mistake that required correction.

adj.—changeable; undependable; unstable

It was a **volatile** situation; no one was willing to bet how things would turn out.

adj.—causing a violent injury

It was a **traumatic** accident, leaving the driver with a broken vertebra, a smashed wrist, and a concussion.

Questions

NOVEL

*Your Own Answer*_____

CIRCUMLOCUTORY

*Your Own Answer*_____

ZEPHYR

*Your Own Answer*_____

Correct Answers

A559

adj.—new

It was a **novel** idea for the rock group to play classical music.

A560

adj.—being too long, as in a description or expression; a roundabout, indirect, or ungainly way of expressing something

It was a **circumlocutory** documentary that could have been cut to half its running time to say twice as much.

A561

n.—a gentle wind; breeze

It was a beautiful day, with a **zephyr** blowing in from the sea.

Questions

BANAL

*Your Own Answer*_____

PROGENY

*Your Own Answer*_____

DIGRESS

*Your Own Answer*_____

Correct Answers

adj.—trite, without freshness or originality

It was a **banal** suggestion to have the annual picnic in the park since that was where it had been for the past five years.

n.—children; offspring

It is through his **progeny** that his name shall live on.

v.—to stray from the subject; to wander from the topic

It is important to not **digress** from the plan of action.

Questions

Q565

WANTON

Your Own Answer

Q566

IRONIC

Your Own Answer

Q567

INTANGIBLE

Your Own Answer

Correct Answers

A565

adj.—unruly; excessive

It is hard to lose weight when one has a **wanton** desire for sweets.

A566

adj.—contradictory; inconsistent; sarcastic

Is it not **ironic** that Americans will toss out left-over French fries while people around the globe continue to starve?

A567

adj.—incapable of being touched; immaterial

Intangible though it may be, sometimes just knowing that the work you do helps others is re-ward enough.

Questions

Q568

INERT

*Your Own Answer*_____

Q569

FEASIBLE

*Your Own Answer*_____

Q570

INCESSANT

*Your Own Answer*_____

Correct Answers

adj.—not reacting chemically; inactive

Inert gases like krypton and argon can enhance window insulation.

adj.—reasonable; practical

Increased exercise is a **feasible** means of weight loss.

adj.—constant; continual

Incessant rain caused the river to flood over its banks.

Questions

Q571

HERESY

*Your Own Answer*_____

Q572

REALM

*Your Own Answer*_____

Q573

SPORADIC

*Your Own Answer*_____

Correct Answers

A571

n.—opinion contrary to popular belief

In this town it is considered **heresy** to want parking spaces to have meters.

A572

n.—an area; sphere of activity

In the **realm** of health care, the issue of who pays and how is never far from the surface.

A573

adj.—rarely occurring or appearing; intermittent

In the desert, there is usually only **sporadic** rainfall.

Questions

Q574

ABSTINENCE

*Your Own Answer*_____

Q575

OBLIGATORY

*Your Own Answer*_____

Q576

ALLUSION

*Your Own Answer*_____

Correct Answers

A574

n.—the act or process of voluntarily refraining from any action or practice; self-control; chastity

In preparation for the Olympic games, the athletes practiced **abstinence** from red meat and junk food, adhering instead to a menu of pasta and produce.

A575

adj.—mandatory; necessary; legally or morally binding

In order to provide a reliable source of revenue for the government, it is **obligatory** for each citizen to pay taxes.

A576

n.—an indirect reference (often literary); a hint

In modern plays, **allusions** are often made to ancient drama.

Questions

Q577

ABSTEMIOUS

*Your Own Answer*_____

Q578

ANOMALY

*Your Own Answer*_____

Q579

SOLILOQUY

*Your Own Answer*_____

Correct Answers

A577

adj.—sparing in use of food or drink

In many **abstemious** cultures, the people are so thin because of their belief that too much taken into the body leads to contamination of the soul.

A578

n.—an oddity; inconsistency; a deviation from the norm

In a parking lot full of Buicks, Chevys, and Plymouths, the Jaguar was an **anomaly**.

A579

n.—a talk one has with oneself (esp. on stage)

Imagine T. S. Eliot's poem "The Waste Land" performed on stage as a kind of **soliloquy**!

Questions

VALID

*Your Own Answer*_____

LIBERALISM

*Your Own Answer*_____

INDOLENT

*Your Own Answer*_____

Correct Answers

A580

adj.—acceptable; legal
Illness is a **valid** reason for missing school.

A581

n.—believing in personal freedom (favoring reform or progress)
If you believe in **liberalism**, the First Amendment is sacrosanct.

A582

adj.—lazy; inactive
If we find him goofing off one more time, we won't be able to escape the fact that he's **indolent**.

Questions

Q583

HEED

*Your Own Answer*_____

Q584

DOGMATIC

*Your Own Answer*_____

Q585

COHERENT

*Your Own Answer*_____

Correct Answers

A583

v.—to obey; to yield to

If the peasant **heeds** the king's commands, she will be able to keep her land.

A584

adj.—stubborn; biased; opinionated

If I say he's **dogmatic**, he'll say he sticks to his guns.

A585

adj.—sticking together; connected; logical; consistent

If he couldn't make a **coherent** speech, how could he run for office?

Questions

CONTEST

*Your Own Answer*_____

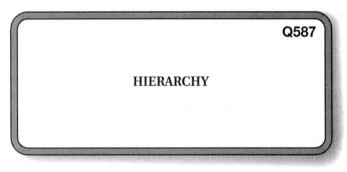

HIERARCHY

*Your Own Answer*_____

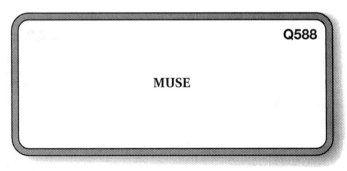

MUSE

*Your Own Answer*_____

Correct Answers

A586

v.—to attempt to disprove or invalidate

I will attempt to **contest** the criminal charges against me.

A587

n.—a system of persons or things arranged according to rank

I was put at the bottom of the **hierarchy**, while Jane was put at the top.

A588

v.—to think or speak meditatively

I expect I'll have to **muse** on that question for a while.

Questions

ILLUMINATE

*Your Own Answer*_____

RAREFY

*Your Own Answer*_____

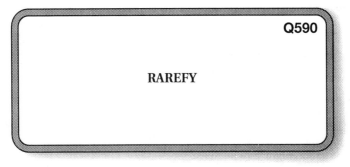

RECLUSE

*Your Own Answer*_____

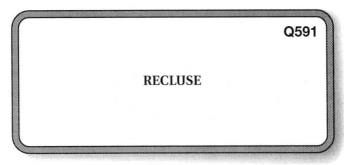

Correct Answers

A589

v.—to make understandable

I asked a classmate to **illuminate** the professor's far-ranging lecture for me.

A590

v.—to make less dense or refined

Hunters were called in to **rarefy** the deer population.

A591

n.—solitary and shut off from society

Howard Hughes, among the most famous and enigmatic figures of the twentieth century, ultimately retreated to a life as a **recluse**.

Questions

RELINQUISH

*Your Own Answer*_____

HEDONISTIC

*Your Own Answer*_____

EXONERATE

*Your Own Answer*_____

Correct Answers

A592

v.—to let go; to abandon

House Speaker Jim Wright had to **relinquish** his position after an ethics investigation undermined his authority.

A593

adj.—pleasure-seeking

Hot tubs, good food, and a plethora of leisure time were hallmarks of this **hedonistic** society.

A594

v.—to declare or prove blameless

Hopefully, the judge will **exonerate** you of any wrongdoing.

Questions

Q595

PLAINTIVE

*Your Own Answer*_____

Q596

ABBREVIATE

*Your Own Answer*_____

Q597

AESTHETIC

*Your Own Answer*_____

Correct Answers

adj.—being mournful or sad

His wife's death made Sam **plaintive**.

v.—to shorten; to compress; to diminish

His vacation to Japan was **abbreviated** when he acquired an illness treatable only in the United States.

adj.—artistic; of beauty; sensitive to beauty

His review made one wonder what kind of **aesthetic** taste the critic had.

Questions

Q598

UNEQUIVOCAL

*Your Own Answer*_____

Q599

PANEGYRIC

*Your Own Answer*_____

Q600

PREVARICATE

*Your Own Answer*_____

Correct Answers

A598

adj.—clear; definite

His response was **unequivocal**, which seemed unusual for a politician.

A599

n.—high praise

His **panegyric** to his opponent stood in sharp contrast to the harsh tenor of the campaign.

A600

v.—to speak equivocally or evasively; to lie

His mother knew no one else could have done it, but the child foolishly **prevaricated** about the stain on the rug.

Questions

Q601

DIFFUSE

*Your Own Answer*_____

Q602

INCISIVE

*Your Own Answer*_____

Q603

PALLID

*Your Own Answer*_____

Correct Answers

A601

adj.—spread out; verbose (wordy); not focused

His monologue was so **diffuse** that all his points were lost.

A602

adj.—to be acute or penetrating

His **incisive** questioning helped settle the matter.

A603

adj.—sallow; colorless

His illness made him **pallid**.

Questions

Q604

TENACIOUS

*Your Own Answer*_____

Q605

GRANDIOSE

*Your Own Answer*_____

Q606

FRUGALITY

*Your Own Answer*_____

Correct Answers

adj.—persistently holding to something

His hold on his dreams is as **tenacious** as anyone's I know.

adj.—magnificent; flamboyant

His **grandiose** idea was to rent a plane to fly to Las Vegas for the night.

n.—thrift; economical use or expenditure

His **frugality** limited him to purchasing the item for which he had a coupon.

Questions

ERRATIC

*Your Own Answer*_____

DISPUTATIOUS

*Your Own Answer*_____

RATIONALIZE

*Your Own Answer*_____

Correct Answers

A607

adj.—unpredictable; irregular

His **erratic** behavior was attributed to the shocking news he had received.

A608

adj.—argumentative; inclined to disputes

His **disputatious** streak eventually wore down his fellow Parliament members.

A609

v.—to offer reasons for; to account for on rational grounds

His daughter attempted to **rationalize** why she had dropped out of college, but she could not give any good reasons.

Questions

Q610

COPIOUS

*Your Own Answer*_____

_____

Q611

CAUSTIC

*Your Own Answer*_____

_____

Q612

HINDRANCE

*Your Own Answer*_____

_____

Correct Answers

A610

adj.—full of information

His **copious** notes gave the reporter all of the information needed.

A611

adj.—burning; sarcastic; harsh

His **caustic** sense of humor doesn't go over so well when people don't know what they're in for.

A612

n.—blockage; obstacle

His assistance often seems to be more of a **hindrance** than a help.

Questions

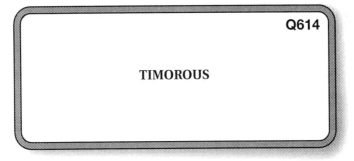

Q613

ABERRANT

*Your Own Answer*_____

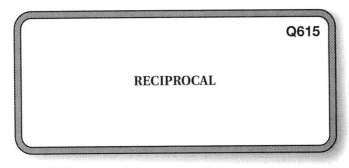

Q614

TIMOROUS

*Your Own Answer*_____

Q615

RECIPROCAL

*Your Own Answer*_____

Correct Answers

A613

adj.— abnormal; straying from the normal or usual path

His **aberrant** behavior led his friends to worry the divorce had taken its toll.

A614

adj.— fearful

Hillary came to accept him as a **timorous** soul who needed succor.

A615

adj.— mutual; having the same relationship to each other

Hernando's membership in the Picture of Health Fitness Center gives him **reciprocal** privileges at 245 health clubs around the U.S.

Questions

INNATE

*Your Own Answer*_____

PRUDENT

*Your Own Answer*_____

PERVADE

*Your Own Answer*_____

Correct Answers

adj.—natural; inborn

Her talent is wondrous: it hardly matters whether it's **innate** or acquired.

adj.—wise; careful; prepared

Her **prudent** ways saved her money, time, and trouble.

v.—to occupy the whole of

Her perfume was so strong that it **pervaded** the whole room.

Questions

Q619

TRIBUTE

*Your Own Answer*_____

_____

Q620

CENSURE

*Your Own Answer*_____

_____

Q621

RESPLENDENT

*Your Own Answer*_____

_____

Correct Answers

A619

n.—expression of admiration

Her performance was a **tribute** to her retiring teacher.

A620

v.—to criticize or disapprove of

Her parents **censured** her idea of dropping out of school.

A621

adj.—dazzling and shining

Her new diamond was **resplendent** in the sunshine.

Questions

TREPIDATION

*Your Own Answer*_____

IMPROMPTU

*Your Own Answer*_____

OBSTINATE

*Your Own Answer*_____

Correct Answers

A622

n.—apprehension; uneasiness

Her long absence caused more than a little **trepidation**.

A623

adj.—without preparation

Her **impromptu** speech was well-received, giving her new confidence in her ability to speak-off-the-cuff.

A624

adj.—stubborn

Her father would not allow her to stay out past midnight; she thought he was **obstinate** because he would not change his mind.

Questions

Q625

GERMANE

*Your Own Answer*_____

Q626

DISAPPROBATION

*Your Own Answer*_____

Q627

DIFFIDENT

*Your Own Answer*_____

Correct Answers

A625

adj.—pertinent; related; to the point

Her essay contained **germane** information, relevant to the new Constitutional amendment.

A626

n.—disapproval

Her **disapprobation** of her daughter's fiancé divided the family.

A627

adj.—timid; lacking self-confidence

Her **diffident** sister couldn't work up the courage to ask for the sale.

Questions

Q628

COMELINESS

*Your Own Answer*_____

Q629

AFFABLE

*Your Own Answer*_____

Q630

PAINSTAKING

*Your Own Answer*_____

Correct Answers

A628

n.—beauty; attractiveness in appearance or behavior

Her **comeliness** attracted many suitors.

A629

adj.—friendly; amiable; good-natured

Her **affable** puppy loved to play with children.

A630

adj.—thorough; careful; precise

Helga's **painstaking** research paid off with a top grade on her essay.

Questions

RHAPSODIZE

*Your Own Answer*_____

AWRY

*Your Own Answer*_____

OPTIMIST

*Your Own Answer*_____

Correct Answers

A631

v.—to speak or write in a very enthusiastic manner

Hearing the general **rhapsodize** about his time as a plebe sent a wave of recognition through the academy grads.

A632

adv.—crooked(ly); uneven(ly); wrong; askew

Hearing the explosion in the laboratory, the scientist realized the experiment had gone **awry**.

A633

n.—person who hopes for the best, sees the good side

He's ever the **optimist**, always seeing the glass as half full.

Questions

Q634

MALINGER

*Your Own Answer*_____

Q635

INSINUATE

*Your Own Answer*_____

Q636

MOROSE

*Your Own Answer*_____

Correct Answers

v.—to pretend to be ill in order to escape work
He will **malinger** on Friday so he can go to the movies.

v.—to work into gradually and indirectly
He will **insinuate** his need for a vacation by saying how tired he has been lately.

adj.—moody, despondent
He was very **morose** over the death of his pet.

Questions

Q637

DEROGATORY

*Your Own Answer*_____

Q638

GAINSAY

*Your Own Answer*_____

Q639

INARTICULATE

*Your Own Answer*_____

Correct Answers

A637

adj.—belittling; uncomplimentary

He was upset because his annual review was full of **derogatory** comments.

A638

v.—to speak against; to contradict; to deny

He was the only one to **gainsay** the law, so it was passed.

A639

adj.—speechless; unable to speak clearly

He was so **inarticulate** that he had trouble making himself understood.

Questions

Q640

ILLUSORY

*Your Own Answer*_____

Q641

PRIVY

*Your Own Answer*_____

Q642

STUPOR

*Your Own Answer*_____

Correct Answers

A640

adj.—unreal; false; deceptive

He was proven guilty when his alibi was found to be **illusory**.

A641

adj.—private; confidential

He was one of a handful of people **privy** to the news of the pending merger.

A642

n.—a stunned or bewildered condition

He was in a **stupor** after being hit on the head.

Questions

DISSEMINATE

*Your Own Answer*_____

VEX

*Your Own Answer*_____

UNPRETENTIOUS

*Your Own Answer*_____

Correct Answers

A643

v.—to circulate; to scatter

He was hired to **disseminate** newspapers to everyone in the town.

A644

v.—to trouble the nerves; to annoy

He was beginning to **vex** her by asking a question every time she passed his locker.

A645

adj.—simple; plain; modest

He was an **unpretentious** farmer: an old John Deere and a beat-up Ford pick-up were all he needed to get the job done.

Questions

VERBATIM

*Your Own Answer*_____

PROSAIC

*Your Own Answer*_____

VINDICATE

*Your Own Answer*_____

Correct Answers

A646

adj.—employing the same words as another; literal

He was accused of plagiarism since he repeated **verbatim** what one of his professors had written many years before.

A647

adj.—tiresome; ordinary

He wanted to do something new; he was tired of the **prosaic** activities his parents suggested each day.

A648

v.—to free from charge; to clear

He **vindicated** the suspect by proving his alibi as truthful.

Questions

Q649

WHEEDLE

*Your Own Answer*_____

_____

Q650

POTENT

*Your Own Answer*_____

_____

Q651

VIGOR

*Your Own Answer*_____

_____

Correct Answers

A649

v.—to try to persuade; to coax

He tried hard to **wheedle** his father into buying him a car.

A650

adj.—having great power or physical strength

He took very **potent** medication and felt better immediately.

A651

n.—energy; forcefulness

He took on the task with great **vigor**, proving his doubters wrong.

Questions

SURMISE

*Your Own Answer*_____

SEETHE

*Your Own Answer*_____

LASCIVIOUS

*Your Own Answer*_____

Correct Answers

v.—to draw an inference; to guess

He **surmised** how the play would end before the second act began.

v.—to be in a state of emotional turmoil; to become angry

He **seethed** at the prospect of losing the business to his conniving uncle.

adj.—indecent; immoral; involving lust

He said it was a harmless pin-up poster, but his mother called it **lascivious**.

Questions

Q655

DEIGN

*Your Own Answer*_____

Q656

REFUTE

*Your Own Answer*_____

Q657

ANACHRONISM

*Your Own Answer*_____

Correct Answers

v.—to condescend; to stoop

He said he wouldn't **deign** to dignify her statement with a response.

v.—to challenge; to disprove

He **refuted** the proposal, deeming it unfair.

n.—something out of place in time (e.g., an airplane in 1492)

He realized that the film about cavemen contained an **anachronism** when he saw a jet cut across the horizon during a hunting scene.

Questions

Q658

DISINTERESTED

*Your Own Answer*_____

Q659

SQUALID

*Your Own Answer*_____

Q660

COGENT

*Your Own Answer*_____

Correct Answers

A658

adj.—neutral; unbiased
He never takes sides; he's always **disinterested**.

A659

adj.—filthy; wretched (from squalor)
He makes good money, but I would never want to work in those **squalid** crawl spaces.

A660

adj.—to the point; clear; convincing in its clarity and presentation
He made a short, **cogent** speech which his audience easily understood.

Questions

LAUD

*Your Own Answer*_____

SERVILE

*Your Own Answer*_____

IDEOLOGY

*Your Own Answer*_____

Correct Answers

A661

v.—to praise
He **lauded** his daughter for winning the trophy.

A662

adj.—slavish; groveling
He knew they both possessed equal abilities, and
yet he was always treated as a **servile** underling.

A663

n.—set of beliefs; principles
He joined the religious group because he agreed
with its **ideology**.

Questions

Q664

PASSIVE

*Your Own Answer*_____

_____

Q665

VIVACIOUS

*Your Own Answer*_____

_____

Q666

BENEFICENT

*Your Own Answer*_____

_____

Correct Answers

A664

adj.—submissive; unassertive
He is so **passive** that others walk all over him.

A665

adj.—animated; gay
He is a great storyteller; his **vivacious** manner makes the tale come to life.

A666

adj.—conferring benefits; kindly; doing good
He is a **beneficent** person, always taking in stray animals and talking to people who need someone to listen.

Questions

INDULGENT

*Your Own Answer*_____

WRY

*Your Own Answer*_____

DISCERNING

*Your Own Answer*_____

Correct Answers

adj.—lenient; patient; permissive

He has **indulgent** tendencies to eat chocolate when he is happy.

adj.—mocking; cynical

He has a **wry** sense of humor which sometimes hurts people's feelings.

adj.—distinguishing one thing from another

He has a **discerning** eye for knowing the original from the copy.

Questions

Q670

CATHARSIS

*Your Own Answer*_____

Q671

ASSIDUOUS

*Your Own Answer*_____

Q672

RANT

*Your Own Answer*_____

A670

n.—a purging or relieving of the body or soul

He experienced a total **catharsis** after the priest absolved his sins.

A671

adj.—carefully attentive; industrious

He enjoys having **assiduous** employees because he can explain a procedure once and have it performed correctly every time.

A672

v.—to speak in a loud, pompous manner; to rave

He disputed the bill with the shipper, **ranting** that he was dealing with thieves.

Questions

DETER

*Your Own Answer*_____

HAPHAZARD

*Your Own Answer*_____

ASPERSION

*Your Own Answer*_____

Correct Answers

A673

v.—to prevent; to discourage; to hinder

He **deterred** the rabbits by putting down garlic around the garden.

A674

adj.—disorganized; random

He constantly misplaced important documents because of his **haphazard** way of running his office.

A675

n.—slanderous statement; a damaging or derogatory criticism

He blamed the loss of his job on an **aspersion** stated by his coworker to his superior.

Questions

Q676

DISINGENUOUS

*Your Own Answer*_____

Q677

SUBSIDIARY

*Your Own Answer*_____

Q678

DEPLETE

*Your Own Answer*_____

Correct Answers

A676

adj.—not frank or candid; deceivingly simple

He always gives a quick, **disingenuous** response; you never get a straight answer.

A677

adj.—subordinate

He acknowledged the importance of the issue, but called it **subsidiary** to a host of other concerns.

A678

v.—to reduce; to empty; to exhaust

Having to pay the entire bill will **deplete** the family's savings.

Questions

TRACTABLE

*Your Own Answer*_____

GULLIBLE

*Your Own Answer*_____

CONFLUENCE

*Your Own Answer*_____

Correct Answers

A679

adj.—easily managed (opposite: intractable)
Having a **tractable** staff made her job a lot easier.

A680

adj.—easily fooled
Gullible people are vulnerable to practical jokes.

A681

n.—a thing that is joined together
Great cities often lie at the **confluence** of great rivers.

Questions

Q682

MYRIAD

*Your Own Answer*_____

Q683

ABSTRACT

*Your Own Answer*_____

Q684

HUMILITY

*Your Own Answer*_____

Correct Answers

A682

adj.—innumerable; countless

Gazing up on the clear, dark midnight sky, the astronomer saw a **myriad** of stars.

A683

adj.—not easy to understand; theoretical

Gauss's law can seem very **abstract** unless you're a mathematician.

A684

n.—lack of pride; modesty

Full of **humility**, she accepted the award but gave all the credit to her mentor.

Questions

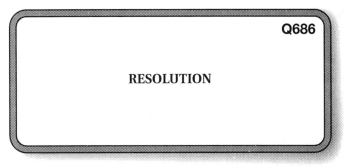

Q685

INFER

*Your Own Answer*_____

Q686

RESOLUTION

*Your Own Answer*_____

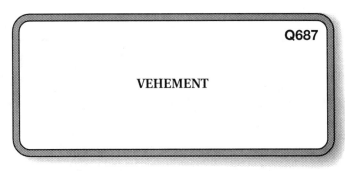

Q687

VEHEMENT

*Your Own Answer*_____

Correct Answers

v.—to form an opinion; to conclude

From the broad outline he supplied, it was easy to **infer** that the applicant knew a great deal about trains.

n.—proposal; promise; determination

Former U.S. Senator George Mitchell journeyed to Ireland to help bring about a peaceful **resolution** to years of strife.

adj.—intense; excited; enthusiastic

Forced by news accounts to make a statement, the talk-show host issued a **vehement** denial of her involvement in the scheme.

Questions

Q688

REPROOF

Your Own Answer _____

Q689

VACUOUS

Your Own Answer _____

Q690

CONSUMMATION

Your Own Answer _____

A688

n.—a rebuke

For all his hard work, all he got was a **reproof** of his efforts.

A689

adj.—dull; stupid; empty-headed

For a time, viewers of TV's *Murphy Brown* looked forward to the seemingly unending parade of **vacuous** secretaries that Murphy went through.

A690

n.—the completion; finish

Following the **consummation** of final exams, most of the students graduated.

Questions

Q691

INCOHERENT

Your Own Answer

Q692

LETHARGIC

Your Own Answer

Q693

PHOBIA

Your Own Answer

Correct Answers

A691

adj.—illogical; rambling; disjointed

Following the accident, the woman went into shock and became **incoherent** as medics struggled to understand her.

A692

adj.—lazy; passive

Feeling very **lethargic**, he watched television or slept the whole day.

A693

n.—morbid fear

Fear of heights is not an uncommon **phobia**.

Questions

Q694

DISHEARTENED

*Your Own Answer*_____

Q695

RUMINATE

*Your Own Answer*_____

Q696

SALUBRIOUS

*Your Own Answer*_____

Correct Answers

A694

adj.—discouraged; depressed
Failing the exam left him **disheartened**.

A695

v.—to think about through meditation
Facing a tough decision, he decided to **ruminate** before making his thoughts known.

A696

adj.—promoting good health
Exercising frequently and eating healthy foods are **salubrious** habits.

Questions

Q697

IMPARTIAL

*Your Own Answer*_____

Q698

TURBULENCE

*Your Own Answer*_____

Q699

INTRACTABLE

*Your Own Answer*_____

Correct Answers

adj.—unbiased; fair

Exasperated by charges to the contrary, the judge reiterated that he had bent over backwards to be **impartial** in a case that crackled with emotion.

n.—condition of being physically agitated; disturbance

Everyone on the plane had to fasten their seat belts as the plane entered an area of **turbulence**.

adj.—stubborn; obstinate; not easily taught or disciplined

Every teacher in the school became frustrated with the **intractable** student and sent him to the principal's office.

Questions

Q700

COTERIE

*Your Own Answer*_____

Q701

IMPASSIVE

*Your Own Answer*_____

Q702

SKEPTIC

*Your Own Answer*_____

A700

n.—a clique; a group who meets frequently, usually socially

Every day after school, she joins her **coterie** on the playground, and they go out for a soda.

A701

adj.—showing no emotion

Even when his father died, he gave an **impassive** response and walked out tearless.

A702

n.—doubter

Even after seeing evidence that his competitor's new engine worked, the engineer remained a **skeptic** that it was marketable.

Questions

Q703

ETHNIC

*Your Own Answer*_____

Q704

EXEMPLARY

*Your Own Answer*_____

Q705

ACCLAIM

*Your Own Answer*_____

Correct Answers

A703

adj.—pertaining to races or peoples and their origin classification or characteristics

Ethnic foods from five continents were set up on the table.

A704

adj.—serving as an example; outstanding

Employees of the month are chosen for their **exemplary** service to the firm.

A705

n.—loud approval; applause

Edward Albee's brilliantly written Broadway revival of *A Delicate Balance* received wide **acclaim**.

Questions

Q706

USURPATION

*Your Own Answer*_____

Q707

ACCRUE

*Your Own Answer*_____

Q708

LANGUID

*Your Own Answer*_____

Correct Answers

A706

n.—the art of taking something for oneself; seizure

During the war, the **usurpation** of the country forced an entirely new culture on the natives.

A707

v.—to collect; to build up

During his many years of collecting stamps, he was able to **accrue** a large collection of valuable items.

A708

adj.—weak; fatigued

During her illness, she was so **languid** she could not leave her bed.

Questions

Q709

PERTINENT

*Your Own Answer*_____

Q710

DEPRAVITY

*Your Own Answer*_____

Q711

DESOLATE

*Your Own Answer*_____

Correct Answers

adj.—related to the matter at hand

During a trial, everyone should concentrate on the same subject, stating only **pertinent** information.

n.—moral corruption; badness

Drugs and money caused **depravity** throughout the once decorous community.

adj.—to be left alone or made lonely

Driving down the **desolate** road had Kelvin worried that he wouldn't reach a gas station in time.

Questions

Q712

NULLIFY

*Your Own Answer*_____

Q713

IMMUNE

*Your Own Answer*_____

Q714

WRATH

*Your Own Answer*_____

Correct Answers

v.—to cancel; to invalidate

Drinking alcohol excessively will **nullify** the positive benefits of eating well and exercising daily.

adj.—exempt from or protected against something

Doesn't everybody wish to be **immune** from the common cold?

n.—violent or unrestrained anger; fury

Do not trespass on his property or you will have to deal with his **wrath**.

Questions

RUMMAGE

*Your Own Answer*_____

DETACHED

*Your Own Answer*_____

DISSONANT

*Your Own Answer*_____

Correct Answers

A715

v.—to search thoroughly

Determined to find his college yearbook, he **rummaged** through every box in the garage.

A716

adj.—separated; not interested; standing alone

Detached from modern conveniences, the islanders live a simple, unhurried life.

A717

adj.—not in harmony; in disagreement

Despite several intense rehearsals, the voices of the choir members continued to be **dissonant**.

Questions

EFFIGY

*Your Own Answer*_____

DELETERIOUS

*Your Own Answer*_____

VULNERABLE

*Your Own Answer*_____

Correct Answers

A718

n.—the image or likeness of a person
Demonstrators carried **effigies** of the dictator they wanted overthrown.

A719

adj.—harmful; hurtful; noxious
Deleterious fumes were traced to the warehouse.

A720

adj.—open to attack; unprotected
Deer usually stay in the forest because they know they are **vulnerable** in open areas.

Questions

Q721

INSIPID

*Your Own Answer*_____

Q722

DECISIVENESS

*Your Own Answer*_____

Q723

SUBLIMINAL

*Your Own Answer*_____

Correct Answers

A721

adj.—uninteresting; bland

Declaring the offerings **insipid**, the critic grudgingly awarded the restaurant one star.

A722

n.—an act of being firm or determined

Decisiveness is one of the key qualities of a successful executive.

A723

adj.—below the level of consciousness

Critics of advertising say that it's loaded with **subliminal** messages.

Questions

NEOPHYTE

*Your Own Answer*_____

_____

ASTRINGENT

*Your Own Answer*_____

_____

ADVERSE

*Your Own Answer*_____

_____

Correct Answers

A724

n.—beginner; newcomer

Critics applauded the **neophyte**'s success and speculated how much better he would get with age and experience.

A725

n.; adj.—1. a substance that contracts bodily tissues 2. causing contraction; tightening; stern; austere

1. After the operation, an **astringent** was used on his skin so that the stretched area would return to normal.
2. The downturn in sales caused the CEO to impose **astringent** measures.

A726

adj.—negative; hostile; antagonistic; inimical

Contrary to the ski resort's expectations, the warm weather generated **adverse** conditions for a profitable weekend.

Questions

RUFFIAN

*Your Own Answer*_____

CONTEMPORARY

*Your Own Answer*_____

DERISION

*Your Own Answer*_____

Correct Answers

A727

n.—tough person or hoodlum

Contrary to popular opinion, **ruffians** are nothing new in the city.

A728

adj.—living or happening at the same time; modern

Contemporary furniture will clash with your traditional sectional.

A729

n.—the act of mocking; ridicule; mockery

Constant **derision** from classmates made him quit school.

Questions

Q730

OBSOLETE

*Your Own Answer*_____

Q731

DICTUM

*Your Own Answer*_____

Q732

CLOYING

*Your Own Answer*_____

Correct Answers

A730

adj.—out of date; passé

Computers have made many formerly manual tasks **obsolete**.

A731

n.—a formal statement of either fact or opinion

Computer programmers have a **dictum**: garbage in, garbage out.

A732

adj.—too sugary; too sentimental or flattering

Complimenting her on her weight loss, clothing, and hairstyle was a **cloying** way to begin asking for a raise.

Questions

Q733

ANALOGY

*Your Own Answer*_____

Q734

PITHY

*Your Own Answer*_____

Q735

CLOTURE

*Your Own Answer*_____

Correct Answers

A733

n.—similarity; correlation; parallelism; simile; metaphor

Comparing the newly discovered virus with one found long ago, the scientist made an **analogy** between the two organisms.

A734

adj.—terse and full of meaning

Columnist William Safire, a former presidential speech writer, has a way with words that often yields **pithy** comments.

A735

n.—a parliamentary procedure to end debate and begin to vote

Cloture was declared as the parliamentarians readied to register their votes.

Questions

VERSATILE

*Your Own Answer*_____

PENURIOUS

*Your Own Answer*_____

PERFUNCTORY

*Your Own Answer*_____

Correct Answers

A736

adj.—having many uses; multifaceted

Clay is a **versatile** material since it can be shaped into so many different objects.

A737

adj.—stingy; miserly

Charles Dickens's Scrooge is the most **penurious** character in any of his tales.

A738

adj.—done in a routine, mechanical way, without interest

Change in career is a good cure for people who have become bored with their occupations and are currently performing their duties in a **perfunctory** fashion.

Questions

Q739

GUILE

*Your Own Answer*_____

Q740

PROVOKE

*Your Own Answer*_____

Q741

ARDUOUS

*Your Own Answer*_____

Correct Answers

A739

n.—slyness; deceit

By using his **guile**, the gambler almost always won.

A740

v.—to stir action or feeling; to arouse

By calling him names, he was **provoking** a fight.

A741

adj.—laborious; difficult; strenuous

Building a house is **arduous** work, but the result is well worth the labor.

Questions

HIATUS

*Your Own Answer*_____

RENEGADE

*Your Own Answer*_____

MINUTE

*Your Own Answer*_____

Correct Answers

A742

n.—interval; break; period of rest

Between graduation and the first day of his new job, Tim took a three-month **hiatus** in the Caribbean.

A743

n.—a person who abandons something such as a religion, cause, or movement; a traitor

Benedict Arnold remains one of the most notorious **renegades** in American history.

A744

adj.—extremely small; tiny

Being on a sodium-restricted diet, he uses only a **minute** amount of salt in his dishes.

Questions

INCOMPATIBLE

*Your Own Answer*_____

KINDLE

*Your Own Answer*_____

TURMOIL

*Your Own Answer*_____

Correct Answers

A745

adj.—disagreeing; disharmonious; not compatible

Being **incompatible** with each other, the children were assigned to sit on opposite sides of the room.

A746

v.—to ignite; to arouse

Being around children **kindled** her interest in educational psychology.

A747

n.—unrest; agitation

Before the country recovered after the war, they experienced a time of great **turmoil**.

Questions

Q748

PERMEABLE

*Your Own Answer*_____

Q749

FICKLE

*Your Own Answer*_____

Q750

JUDICIOUS

*Your Own Answer*_____

Correct Answers

adj.—porous; allowing to pass through

Because the material was **permeable**, the water was able to drain.

adj.—changeable; unpredictable

Because the man was **fickle**, he could not be trusted to make a competent decision.

adj.—to have or show sound judgment

Because the elder was **judicious**, the tough decisions were left to him.

Questions

LABYRINTH

*Your Own Answer*_____

PRESCRIPTIVE

*Your Own Answer*_____

COALESCE

*Your Own Answer*_____

Correct Answers

A751

n.—maze

Be careful not to get lost in the **labyrinth** of vegetation.

A752

adj.—done by custom; unbending

At the heart of the Australian aborigines' **prescriptive** coming-of-age rite for men is a walkabout.

A753

v.—to combine; to come together

At the end of the conference, the five groups **coalesced** in one room.

Questions

Q754

PARADOX

*Your Own Answer*_____

Q755

RELEVANT

*Your Own Answer*_____

Q756

REVERIE

*Your Own Answer*_____

Correct Answers

A754

n.—a tenet seemingly contradictory or false, but actually true

At first blush, the company's results were a **paradox**: sales were down, yet profits were up.

A755

adj.—of concern; significant

Asking applicants about their general health is **relevant** since much of the job requires physical strength.

A756

n.—the condition of being unaware of one's surroundings; trance; dreamy thinking or imagining, especially of agreeable things

As their anniversary neared, Liane fell into a **reverie** as she recalled all the good times she and Roscoe had had.

Questions

INGENUE

*Your Own Answer*_____

_____

SUCCINCT

*Your Own Answer*_____

_____

LAGGARD

*Your Own Answer*_____

_____

A757

n.—an unworldly young woman

As an **ingenue**, Corky had no experience outside of her small town.

A758

adj.—consisting of few words; concise

Articles in *USA Today* are so **succinct** that some observers nicknamed the newspaper "McPaper."

A759

n.—a lazy person; one who lags behind

Anything can happen in a swim meet: last year's leader can become this year's **laggard**.

Questions

DILIGENCE

*Your Own Answer*_____

STAMINA

*Your Own Answer*_____

EVOKE

*Your Own Answer*_____

Correct Answers

A760

n.—hard work

Anything can be accomplished with **diligence** and commitment.

A761

n.—endurance

Anybody who can finish the New York Marathon has lots of **stamina**.

A762

v.—to call forth; to elicit

Announcement of the results **evoked** a cheer from the crowd.

Questions

Q763

ANIMOSITY

*Your Own Answer*_____

Q764

INQUISITIVE

*Your Own Answer*_____

Q765

IMPLICATION

*Your Own Answer*_____

Correct Answers

A763

n.—a feeling of hatred or ill will

Animosity grew between the two feuding families.

A764

adj.—eager to ask questions in order to learn

An **inquisitive** youngster is likely to become a wise adult.

A765

n.—suggestion; inference

An **implication** was made that there might be trickery involved.

Questions

Q766

AUTHENTIC

*Your Own Answer*_____

_____

Q767

BENEFACTOR

*Your Own Answer*_____

_____

Q768

MANIFEST

*Your Own Answer*_____

_____

Correct Answers

A766

adj.—real; genuine; trustworthy
An **authentic** diamond will cut glass.

A767

n.—one who helps others; a donor
An anonymous **benefactor** donated $10,000 to
the children's hospital.

A768

adj.—obvious; clear
America's **manifest** destiny was to acquire all of
the land between the Pacific and Atlantic Oceans.

Questions

SUPERFLUOUS

*Your Own Answer*_____

MOTIF

*Your Own Answer*_____

PREDECESSOR

*Your Own Answer*_____

Correct Answers

A769

adj.—unnecessary; extra

Although the designer considered the piece **superfluous**, the woman wanted the extra chair in her bedroom.

A770

n.—theme

Although the college students lived in Alaska, they decided on a tropical **motif** for their dorm room.

A771

n.—one who has occupied an office before another

Although her **predecessor** did not accomplish any goals that would help the poor, the new mayor was confident that she could finally help those in need.

Questions

Q772

TRIVIAL

*Your Own Answer*_____

Q773

MENTOR

*Your Own Answer*_____

Q774

DISSEMBLE

*Your Own Answer*_____

Correct Answers

A772

adj.—unimportant; small; worthless

Although her mother felt otherwise, she considered her dishwashing chore **trivial**.

A773

n.—teacher; wise and faithful advisor

Alan consulted his **mentor** when he needed critical advice.

A774

v.—to disguise and conceal

Agent 007 has a marvelous ability to **dissemble** his real intentions.

Questions

Q775

PHILANTHROPY

*Your Own Answer*_____

Q776

BURGEON

*Your Own Answer*_____

Q777

VERTIGO

*Your Own Answer*_____

Correct Answers

n.—charity; unselfishness

After years of donating time and money to the children's hospital, Mrs. Elderwood was commended for her **philanthropy**.

v.—to grow or develop quickly

After the first punch was thrown, the dispute **burgeoned** into a brawl.

n.—dizziness

After spinning around for five minutes, he experienced **vertigo**.

Questions

BALEFUL

*Your Own Answer*_____

DISPARAGE

*Your Own Answer*_____

SAVOR

*Your Own Answer*_____

Correct Answers

A778

adj.—harmful; malignant; detrimental

After she was fired, she realized it was a **baleful** move to point the blame at her superior.

A779

v.—to belittle; to undervalue

After she fired him, she realized that she had **disparaged** the value of his assistance.

A780

v.—to receive pleasure from; to enjoy with appreciation; to dwell on with delight

After several months without a day off, she **savored** every minute of her week-long vacation.

Questions

LARCENY

*Your Own Answer*_____

SURPASS

*Your Own Answer*_____

ARROGANT

*Your Own Answer*_____

Correct Answers

A781

n.—theft; stealing

After robbing the liquor store, she was found guilty of **larceny**.

A782

v.—to go beyond; to outdo

After recovering from a serious illness, the boy **surpassed** the doctor's expectations by leaving the hospital two days early.

A783

adj.—acting superior to others; conceited

After purchasing his new, expensive sports car, the **arrogant** doctor refused to allow anyone to ride with him to the country club.

Questions

Q784

INFAMOUS

Your Own Answer_____

Q785

DEFERENTIAL

Your Own Answer_____

Q786

KNEAD

Your Own Answer_____

Correct Answers

A784

adj.—having a bad reputation; notorious

After producing machines that developed many problems, the production company became **infamous** for poor manufacturing.

A785

adj.—yielding to the opinion of another

After months of debating students' needs in the Sixth Ward, the mayor's **deferential** statements indicated that he had found some common ground with them.

A786

v.—to mix; to massage

After mixing the ingredients, the baker **kneaded** the dough and set it aside to rise.

Questions

Q787

PROVINCIAL

*Your Own Answer*_____

Q788

BOMBAST

*Your Own Answer*_____

Q789

DENIGRATE

*Your Own Answer*_____

Correct Answers

A787

adj.—regional; unsophisticated

After living in the city for five years, he found that his family back home on the farm was too **provincial** for his cultured ways.

A788

n.—pompous speech; pretentious words

After he delivered his **bombast** at the podium, he arrogantly left the meeting.

A789

v.—to defame; to blacken or sully; to belittle

After finding out her evil secret, he announced it to the council and **denigrated** her in public.

Questions

Q790

SCRUPULOUS

*Your Own Answer*_____

Q791

ABSOLVE

*Your Own Answer*_____

Q792

PESSIMISM

*Your Own Answer*_____

Correct Answers

A790

adj.—honorable; exact

After finding a purse with valuable items inside, the **scrupulous** Mr. Prendergast returned everything to its owner.

A791

v.—to forgive; to acquit

After feuding for many years, the brothers **absolved** each other for the many arguments they had.

A792

n.—seeing only the gloomy side; hopelessness

After endless years of drought, **pessimism** grew in the hearts of even the most dedicated farmers.

Questions

Q793

SCRUTINIZE

*Your Own Answer*_____

Q794

QUIESCENCE

*Your Own Answer*_____

Q795

ACQUIESCE

*Your Own Answer*_____

Correct Answers

A793

v.—to examine closely; to study

After allowing his son to borrow the family car, the father **scrutinized** every section for dents.

A794

n.—state of being at rest or without motion

After a tough day on the shipping dock, one needs **quiescence**.

A795

v.—to agree without protest

After a hard-fought battle, the retailers finally **acquiesced** to the draft regulations.

Questions

ACCOLADE

*Your Own Answer*_____

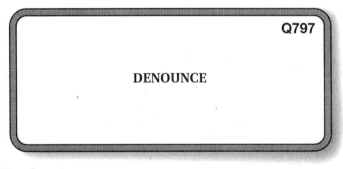

DENOUNCE

*Your Own Answer*_____

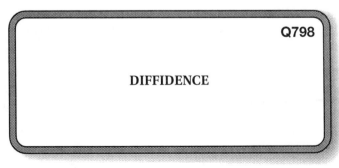

DIFFIDENCE

*Your Own Answer*_____

Correct Answers

A796

n.—a sign of approval or respect

Accolades flowed into her dressing room following the opening-night triumph.

A797

v.—to speak out against; to condemn

A student rally was called to **denounce** the use of drugs on campus.

A798

n.—a hesitation in asserting oneself

A shy person may have great **diffidence** when faced with a problem.

Questions

Q799

SHADY

*Your Own Answer*_____

Q800

ALTERCATION

*Your Own Answer*_____

Q801

DEARTH

*Your Own Answer*_____

Correct Answers

A799

adj.—a character of questionable honesty

A **shady** person would not be trusted with a sensitive secret.

A800

n.—controversy; dispute

A serious **altercation** caused the marriage to end in a bitter divorce.

A801

n.—scarcity; shortage

A series of coincidental resignations left the firm with a **dearth** of talent.

Questions

Q802

SECTARIAN

Your Own Answer insular, parochial
both mean narrow minded

Q803

CHICANERY

*Your Own Answer*_____

Q804

TACITURN

*Your Own Answer*_____

Correct Answers

A802

adj.—to be narrow-minded or limited

A **sectarian** speaker precluded him from listening to the other side.

A803

n.—trickery or deception

A news broadcast is no place for **chicanery**.

A804

adj.—inclined to silence; speaking little; dour; stern

A mime may be **taciturn**, but his performance can speak volumes.

Questions

Q805

APPEASE

*Your Own Answer*_____

Q806

METAMORPHOSIS

*Your Own Answer*_____

Q807

ANOINT

*Your Own Answer*_____

Correct Answers

A805

v.—to satisfy; to calm

A milk bottle usually **appeases** a crying baby.

A806

n.—change of form

A **metamorphosis** caused the caterpillar to become a beautiful butterfly.

A807

v.—to crown; to ordain

A member of the monarchy was **anointed** by the king.

Questions

Q808

BENIGN

*Your Own Answer*_____

Q809

HYPOTHETICAL

*Your Own Answer*_____

Q810

EFFEMINATE

*Your Own Answer*_____

Correct Answers

A808

adj.—mild; harmless

A lamb is a **benign** animal, especially when compared with a lion.

A809

adj.—assumed; uncertain; conjectural

A **hypothetical** situation was set up so we could practice our responses.

A810

adj.—having qualities attributed to a woman; delicate

A high-pitched laugh made the man seem **effeminate**.

Questions

PRECLUDE

*Your Own Answer*_____

LITHE

Lissome

Your Own Answer Cirque de So LITHE

GOURMAND

*Your Own Answer*_____

Correct Answers

A811

v.—to inhibit; to make impossible

A healthy diet and lifestyle will not **preclude** you from getting ill, although it improves your immune system.

A812

adj.—to be limber or supple

A gymnast needs to be **lithe** in order to do a split.

A813

n.—one who eats eagerly

A **gourmand** may eat several servings of entree.

Questions

Q814

DEFENSIBLE

*Your Own Answer*_____

Q815

FOSTER

*Your Own Answer*_____

Q816

ATROPHY

*Your Own Answer*_____

Correct Answers

A814

adj.—that which can be justified
A good strategy needs to be **defensible**.

A815

v.—to encourage; to nurture; to support
A good practice routine **fosters** success.

A816

v.—to waste away, as from lack of use; to wither
A few months after he lost his ability to walk, his legs began to **atrophy**.

Questions

FINESSE

*Your Own Answer*_____

OBVIATE

*Your Own Answer*_____

CURB

*Your Own Answer*_____

Correct Answers

A817

n.—the ability to handle situations with skill and diplomacy

A diplomat with great **finesse**, Madeleine Albright was destined for high office.

A818

v.—to make unnecessary

A cure for the common cold would **obviate** the need for shelf after shelf of cold remedies.

A819

n.—a restraint or framework

A **curb** was put up along the street to help drainage.

Questions

Q820

INHERENT

*Your Own Answer*_____

Q821

INEVITABLE

*Your Own Answer*_____

Q822

CITADEL

*Your Own Answer*_____

Correct Answers

A820

adj.—part of the essential character; intrinsic

A constant smile is **inherent** in pageant competitors.

A821

adj.—sure to happen; unavoidable

A confrontation between the disagreeing neighbors seemed **inevitable**.

A822

n.—a fortress set up high to defend a city

A **citadel** sat on the hill to protect the city below.

Questions

Q823

BILATERAL

*Your Own Answer*_____

Q824

CODDLE

*Your Own Answer*_____

Q825

OPULENCE

*Your Own Answer*_____

Correct Answers

A823

adj.—pertaining to or affecting both sides or two sides; having two sides

A **bilateral** decision was made so that both partners reaped equal benefits from the same amount of work.

A824

v.—to treat with tenderness

A baby needs to be **coddled**.

A825

n.—wealth; fortune

A 40-room mansion on 65 wooded acres is only the most visible sign of her **opulence**.

Questions

Q826

HARBOR

*Your Own Answer*_____

Q827

ACERBIC

*Your Own Answer*_____

Q828

CRASS

*Your Own Answer*_____

Correct Answers

A826

n.; v.—1. a place of safety or shelter 2. to give shelter or to protect

1. We stood at the dock as the ship sailed into the **harbor**.
2. The peasants were executed for **harboring** known rebels.

A827

adj.—1. tasting sour 2. harsh in language or temper

1. Too much bay leaf will make the eggplant **acerbic**.
2. The columnist's **acerbic** comments about the First Lady drew a strong denunciation from the President.

A828

adj.—1. stupid or dull; insensitive 2. materialistic

1. To make light of someone's weakness is **crass**.
2. They made their money the old-fashioned way, but still they were accused of being **crass**.

Questions

Q829

DOCUMENT

*Your Own Answer*_____

Q830

AFFINITY

*Your Own Answer*_____

Q831

EFFERVESCENCE

*Your Own Answer*_____

Correct Answers

A829

n.; v.—1. official paper containing information 2. to support; to substantiate; to verify

1. They needed a written **document** to prove that the transaction occurred.
2. Facing an audit, she had to **document** all her client contacts.

A830

n.—1. a connection 2. similarity of structure

1. There is a strong emotional **affinity** between the two siblings.
2. It turns out that the elements bear a strong **affinity** to each other.

A831

n.—1. liveliness; spirit 2. bubbliness

1. The woman's **effervescence** was a delightful change.
2. The cream soda's **effervescence** tickled my nose.

Questions

Q832

SPURN

*Your Own Answer*_____

Q833

PARTISAN

*Your Own Answer*_____

Q834

CACHE

*Your Own Answer*_____

Correct Answers

A832

v.; n.—1. to push away 2. a strong rejection

1. The woman **spurned** the advances of her suitor, saying she wasn't ready for a commitment.
2. Unlucky enough to be the ninth telemarketer to call Jane that evening, he caught her **spurn**.

A833

n.; adj.—1. supporter; follower 2. biased; one-sided

1. The union president is a **partisan** of minimum-wage legislation.
2. Republican U.S. Senator Alfonse D'Amato was accused by Democrats of having **partisan** motives in the zeal with which he pursued hearings on the Whitewater Affair.

A834

n.—1. stockpile 2. hiding place for goods

1. The town kept a **cache** of salt on hand to melt winter's snow off the roads.
2. Extra food is kept in the **cache** under the pantry.

Questions

Q835

FACADE

*Your Own Answer*_____

Q836

CONJURE

*Your Own Answer*_____

Q837

ROUT

*Your Own Answer*_____

Correct Answers

A835

n.—1. false appearance 2. front view of a building

1. The smile on her face was only a **facade** for her true feelings of sorrow.
2. The building's **facade** was faded and aging.

A836

v.— 1. to call upon or appeal to 2. to cause to be, appear, or become

1. The smell of the dinner **conjured** images of childhood.
2. The magician **conjured** a rabbit out of a hat.

A837

n.; v.— 1. a noisy or disorderly crowd 2. a retreat or terrible defeat 3. to dig up

1. The **rout** kept the police busy all morning with crowd control.
2. The Scarlet Knights beat the Fighting Irish in a **rout**, 56-14.
3. I need to **rout** the backyard in order to put in the pipes.

Questions

Q838

ALLURE

*Your Own Answer*_____

Q839

CONFOUND

*Your Own Answer*_____

Q840

PONDEROUS

*Your Own Answer*_____

Correct Answers

A838

v.; n.— 1. to attract; to entice 2. attraction; temptation; glamour

1. The romantic young man **allured** the beautiful woman by preparing a wonderful dinner.
2. Singapore's **allure** is its bustling economy.

A839

v.—1. to lump together causing confusion 2. to damn

1. The problem **confounded** our ability to solve it.
2. **Confound** you, you scoundrel!

A840

adj.—1. unwieldy from weight 2. dull or labored

1. The **ponderous** piano posed a serious challenge to having it pulled up to the 16th floor.
2. As if being grainy wasn't bad enough, the film's **ponderous** story made it tough to get through.

Questions

PARODY

*Your Own Answer*_____

DISPERSE

*Your Own Answer*_____

ASCETIC

*Your Own Answer*_____

Correct Answers

A841

n.—1. a piece of work imitating another in a satirical manner 2. a poor imitation

1. The play was a **parody** of the prince and princess's marital difficulties.
2. Ugh! This is a **parody** of a fashionable dress!

A842

v.—1. to scatter 2. to separate

1. The pilots **dispersed** the food drops over a wide area of devastation.
2. Tear gas was used to **disperse** the crowd.

A843

n.; adj.— 1. one who leads a simple life of self-denial 2. rigorously abstinent

1. The monastery is filled with **ascetics** who have devoted their lives to religion.
2. The nuns lead an **ascetic** life devoted to the Lord.

Questions

INCLINED

*Your Own Answer*_____

OBTUSE

*Your Own Answer*_____

MACULATE

*Your Own Answer*_____

Correct Answers

A844

adj.—1. apt to; likely 2. angled

1. The man's ear for music indicated he was **inclined** toward learning an instrument.
2. The hillside was **inclined** just enough to make for a fairly serious climb.

A845

adj.—1. dull 2. greater than 90° but less than 180° 3. slow to understand or perceive

1. The man was so **obtuse**, he even made the dog yawn.
2. The textbook problem asks the reader to solve for the **obtuse** angle.
3. He's **obtuse** when it comes to abstract art.

A846

adj.; v.—1. spotted; blotched; defiled; impure (opposite: immaculate) 2. to stain; to spot; to defile

1. The **maculate** rug could not be cleaned.
2. Grape juice **maculated** the carpet.

Questions

LUCID

*Your Own Answer*_____

AGHAST

*Your Own Answer*_____

REND

*Your Own Answer*_____

Correct Answers

A847

adj.—1. shining 2. easily understood

1. The **lucid** quarter was easily spotted.
2. Lincoln's Gettysburg Address was artful, yet **lucid**.

A848

adj.—1. astonished; amazed 2. horrified; terrified; appalled

1. The landlord was **aghast** at his water bill.
2. The children's **aghast** expressions were indicative of the frightening experience they had on the amusement ride.

A849

v.— 1. to rip cr pull from 2. to split with violence 3. to disturb with a sharp noise

1. The kidnapper **rent** the newborn baby from the arms of its mother as she was leaving the hospital.
2. A freakish water spout **rent** the fishing boat in half.
3. Every morning, the 5:47 local out of New Brunswick **rends** the dawn's silence with its air horn.

Questions

DELIBERATE

*Your Own Answer*_____

RABID

*Your Own Answer*_____

CASCADE

*Your Own Answer*_____

Correct Answers

A850

v.; adj.—1. to consider carefully; weigh in the mind 2. intentional

1. The jury **deliberated** for three days before reaching a verdict.
2. The brother's **deliberate** attempt to get his sibling blamed for his mistake was obvious to all.

A851

adj.; n.— 1. furious; with extreme anger 2. a disease affecting animals

1. The insult made him **rabid**.
2. Discovering that the dog was **rabid**, the mail carrier knew he'd have to get a shot after he was bitten.

A852

n.; v.—1. waterfall 2. to pour; to rush; to fall

1. The hikers stopped along the path to take in the beauty of the rushing **cascade**.
2. The water **cascaded** down the rocks into the pool.

Questions

CLEMENCY

*Your Own Answer*_____

PROGRAM

*Your Own Answer*_____

VAGRANT

*Your Own Answer*_____

Correct Answers

A853

n.— 1. mercy toward an offender 2. mildness

1. The governor granted the prisoner **clemency**.
2. The weather's **clemency** made for a perfect picnic.

A854

n.— 1. the parts of entertainment 2. a plan for dealing with a matter 3. coded instructions

1. The free-form music **program** on Sunday nights is virtually unique in commercial radio.
2. The **program** for better health is to eat more vegetables and fruits.
3. The store's computer **program** allows sale information to prompt at the register for certain items at certain hours.

A855

n.; adj.— 1. homeless person 2. rambling; wandering; transient

1. The first thing the shop owner did every morning was chase a **vagrant** from her doorstep.
2. Circus performers, with nary an opportunity to put down roots, typically lead a **vagrant** life.

Questions

Q856

TORTUOUS

Your Own Answer Sinuous Road
Tortuous Road up to Cant Olof

Q857

JARGON

Your Own Answer

Q858

INUNDATE

Your Own Answer

Correct Answers

A856

adj.—1. full of twists and turns 2. deceitful

1. The course for the 10K race proved **tortuous**, with most of the turns keeping the runners within view of the shoreline.

2. Emilio gave a **tortuous** explanation for his whereabouts the night before, and his wife furrowed her brow in disbelief.

A857

n.—1. incoherent speech 2. specialized vocabulary in certain fields

1. The conversation was nothing but **jargon**, but then the speakers were nothing but cartoon characters who specialize in an oddly bracing form of gibberish.

2. The engineers' **jargon** is indecipherable to a layperson.

A858

v.—1. to flood 2. to overwhelm with a large amount of

1. The broken water main **inundated** the business district with water.

2. Surfing the Internet can **inundate** you with information, which is why a Web browser comes in handy.

Questions

Q859

LAMENT

*Your Own Answer*_____

Q860

BLATANT

*Your Own Answer*_____

Q861

BIENNIAL

*Your Own Answer*_____

Correct Answers

v.; n.—1. to mourn or grieve 2. expression of grief or sorrow

1. The boy is **lamenting** the loss of his pet.
2. Pedro's only **lament** was that his wife didn't outlive him.

adj.—1. obvious; unmistakable 2. crude; vulgar

1. The **blatant** foul was reason for ejection.
2. The defendant was **blatant** in his testimony.

adj.; n.— 1. happening every two years 2. a plant which blooms every two years

1. The **biennial** journal's influence seemed only magnified by its infrequent publication.
2. She has lived here for four years and has seen the **biennials** bloom twice.

Questions

Q862

AUTHORITARIAN

*Your Own Answer*_____

Q863

ZENITH

*Your Own Answer*_____

Q864

MATERIALISM

*Your Own Answer*_____

Correct Answers

A862

n.; adj.— 1. acting as a dictator 2. demanding obedience

1. The **authoritarian** made all of the rules but did none of the work.
2. Fidel Castro is reluctant to give up his **authoritarian** rule.

A863

n.—1. point directly overhead in the sky 2. highest point

1. The astronomer pointed her telescope straight up toward the **zenith**.
2. The Broncos seemed to be at the **zenith** of their power just as their rivals on the turf were flagging.

A864

n.— 1. the belief that everything in the universe is explained in terms of matter 2. the belief that worldly possessions are the be-all and end-all in life

1. Spiritualists will tell you that **materialism** is only half the story.
2. Some said that the prince's profligacy gave **materialism** a bad name.

Questions

DISDAIN

*Your Own Answer*_____

DEMUR

*Your Own Answer*_____

TEMPER

*Your Own Answer*_____

Correct Answers

A865

n.; v.— 1. intense dislike 2. to look down upon; to scorn

1. She showed great **disdain** toward anyone who did not agree with her.
2. She **disdains** the very ground you walk upon.

A866

v.; n.— 1. to object 2. objection; misgiving

1. She hated animals, so when the subject of buying a cat came up, she **demurred**.
2. She said yes, but he detected a **demur** in her voice.

A867

v.—1. to moderate, as by mingling with something else 2. to bring to the proper condition by treatment

1. She drew a hot bath, but then realized she'd have to **temper** it with a little cool water or end up scalded.
2. The craftsman **tempered** the steel before being able to twist it to form a table leg.

Questions

Q868

DITHER

*Your Own Answer*_____

Q869

AMISS

*Your Own Answer*_____

Q870

DIDACTIC

Your Own Answer instructive or dogmatic

Correct Answers

v.; n.— 1. to act indecisively 2. a confused condition

1. She **dithered** every time she had to make a decision.
2. Having to take two tests in one day left the student in a **dither**.

adj.; adv.—1. wrong; awry 2. wrongly; in a defective manner

1. Seeing that his anorak was gone, he knew something was **amiss**.
2. Its new muffler aside, the car was behaving **amiss**.

adj.—1. instructive 2. dogmatic; preachy

1. Our teacher's **didactic** technique boosted our scores.
2. The **didactic** activist was not one to be swayed.

Questions

Q871

RECESSION

*Your Own Answer*_____

Q872

PHENOMENON

*Your Own Answer*_____

Q873

QUIRK

*Your Own Answer*_____

Correct Answers

A871

n.—1. withdrawal 2. economic downturn

1. Oscar's gum **recession** left him with sensitive teeth.

2. Soaring unemployment in the nation's industrial belt triggered **recession**.

A872

n.—1. exceptional person 2. unusual occurrence

1. They call Yankee Stadium "The House that Ruth Built" because the Babe was a **phenomenon**.

2. The northern lights are a rare **phenomenon** for those not living near the Arctic Circle.

A873

n.—1. peculiar behavior 2. startling twist

1. Nobody's perfect—we all have our **quirks**.

2. Our vacation went smoothly save for one **quirk**—a hurricane that came barreling into the coastline as we were preparing to head home.

Questions

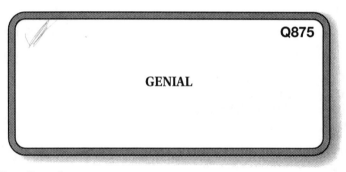

Q874

MERCENARY

*Your Own Answer*_____

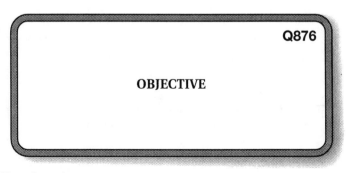

Q875

GENIAL

*Your Own Answer*_____

Q876

OBJECTIVE

*Your Own Answer*_____

Correct Answers

A874

adj.; n.— 1. working or done for payment only
2. hired (soldier)

1. Lila was suspicious that Joe had jumped at the chance only for **mercenary** reasons.
2. A **mercenary** was hired for a hundred dollars a month, good money in those days even if you had to fight a war to get it.

A875

adj.— 1. contributing to life 2. amiable

1. Key West's **genial** climate is among its many attractive aspects.
2. Her **genial** personality made her a favorite party guest.

A876

adj.; n.— 1. open-minded; impartial 2. goal

1. It's hard to set aside your biases and be **objective**.
2. The law student decided that her primary **objective** after graduation was to pass the Bar examination.

Questions

Q877

ARTICULATE

*Your Own Answer*_____

Q878

RAZE

*Your Own Answer*_____

Q879

VIABLE

*Your Own Answer*_____

Correct Answers

A877

v.; adj.—1. to utter clearly and distinctly 2. clear; distinct; expressed with clarity; skillful with words

1. It's even more important to **articulate** your words when you're on the phone.
2. You didn't have to vote for him to agree that Adlai Stevenson was **articulate**.

A878

v.—1. to scrape, as in wound 2. to demolish

1. It must be time to give the cat a manicure; she **razed** my skin last night.
2. They will **raze** the old Las Vegas hotel to make room for a $2.5 billion gambling palace.

A879

adj.— 1. capable of maintaining life 2. possible; attainable

1. Is life **viable** on Mars?
2. It was deemed a **viable** option because the city did have the funds to support it.

Questions

PROVOCATIVE

*Your Own Answer*_____

RHETORICAL

*Your Own Answer*_____

MALIGN

*Your Own Answer*_____

Correct Answers

A880

adj.—1. tempting 2. irritating

1. In the movie *Roger Rabbit*, the animated Jessica Rabbit demurs when she's told she's **provocative**, saying that she's only drawn that way.
2. The U.S. considered the invasion of Kuwait a **provocative** action.

A881

adj.—1. having to do with verbal communication 2. artificial eloquence

1. In posing a **rhetorical** question, he hoped to get people thinking.
2. The perception that Gary Hart was spouting **rhetorical** flourishes enabled fellow Democrat Walter Mondale to score debate points by asking, "Where's the beef?"

A882

v.; adj.—1. to speak evil of 2. having an evil disposition toward others (opposite: benign)

1. In her statement to the judge, she **maligned** her soon-to-be ex-husband.
2. She had such a **malign** personality that no one even tried to approach her, mostly out of fear.

Questions

Q883

IMPLEMENT

*Your Own Answer*_____

_____

Q884

PROPENSITY

*Your Own Answer*_____

_____

Q885

CONSEQUENTIAL

*Your Own Answer*_____

_____

Correct Answers

A883

v.; n.—1. to carry into effect 2. something used in a given activity

1. In case of emergency, **implement** the evacuation plan immediately.
2. The rack is an **implement** of torture.

A884

n.—1. a natural tendency towards 2. bias

1. I have a **propensity** to talk too fast.
2. She has a **propensity** to hire men over women.

A885

adj.—1. following as an effect 2. important

1. His long illness and **consequential** absence set him behind in his homework.
2. The decision to move the company will be **consequential** to its success.

Questions

Q886

HONE

Your Own Answer Many of the troops hone to be home with their family

---

Q887

RESIGNATION

Your Own Answer

Q888

INITIATE

Your Own Answer

Correct Answers

A886

v.—1. to sharpen, as with a stone 2. to long or yearn for

1. He's still **honing** his skills at the potter's wheel.
2. The traveler **hones** for his homeland.

A887

n.—1. quitting 2. submission

1. He submitted his **resignation** because he found a new job.
2. You could see the **resignation** on his face: Things just weren't working out as he had expected.

A888

v.; n.—1. to begin; to admit into a group 2. a person who is in the process of being admitted into a group

1. He **initiated** the dinner discussion by asking his father to borrow the car.
2. As an **initiate** to the Explorers, George was expected to have a taste for the outdoor life.

Questions

SANGUINE

*Your Own Answer*_____

COGNATE

Your Own Answer Gary is a cognate from my mom's side

NOTORIOUS

*Your Own Answer*_____

Correct Answers

A889

adj.—1. optimistic; cheerful 2. red

1. Even when victory seemed impossible, the general remained **sanguine**.

2. The dress was **sanguine** with a bright green border stripe.

A890

adj.; n.— 1. having the same family 2. a person related through ancestry

1. English and German are **cognate** languages.

2. The woman was a **cognate** to the royal family.

A891

adj.—1. infamous; renowned 2. having an unfavorable connotation

1. Discovering that her new neighbor was **notorious** for thievery, she decided to purchase an alarm system for her home.

2. The criminal had a **notorious** reputation.

Questions

Q892

PAROCHIAL

Your Own Answer sectarian- narrow minded
insular - narrow minded

Q893

IMPETUOUS

*Your Own Answer*_____

Q894

WRETCHED

*Your Own Answer*_____

Correct Answers

adj.—1. religious 2. narrow-minded

1. Devout Christians, the Chesterfields enrolled their children in a **parochial** school.

2. Governor Kean urged Republicans to rise above **parochial** interests and be the party of inclusion.

adj.—1. rash; impulsive 2. forcible; violent

1. Dagmar came to regret his **impetuous** actions, once he realized what he'd done.

2. The pirate's men boarded the ship with **impetuous** matter-of-factness.

adj.—1. miserable or unhappy 2. causing distress

1. Brought up in an orphanage, Annie led a **wretched** existence.

2. The continual rain made for a **wretched** vacation.

Questions

Q895

PIQUE

Your Own Answer Tangy has a right to feel pique.
She was overlooked for the pomotion because they
brought someone else in from outside the company

Q896

MAGNANIMITY

---

*Your Own Answer*_____

Q897

DISCRIMINATE

---

*Your Own Answer*_____

Correct Answers

n.; v.—1. resentment at being slighted 2. to provoke

1. Being passed over for the promotion aroused his **pique**.
2. The more he **piqued** her, the redder she grew.

n.; adj.—1. a quality of nobleness of mind, disdain of meanness or revenge 2. forgiving; unselfish

1. Being full of **magnanimity**, he asked the thief only for an apology and set him free.
2. The **magnanimous** store owner did not press charges once an apology was given.

v.; adj.—1. to distinguish 2. demonstrating bias

1. Being a chef, he **discriminated** carefully among ingredients.
2. Reeling from the fact that senior managers had been caught on tape making offensive remarks, the CEO said he would not tolerate any of his firm's employees **discriminating** against anyone for any reason.

Questions

Q898

ADVOCATE

*Your Own Answer*_____

Q899

PLAUSIBLE

*Your Own Answer*_____

Q900

INSULAR

Your Own Answer parochial - narrow minded

Sectarian - narrow minded

Correct Answers

A898

v.; n.—1. to plead in favor of 2. supporter; defender

1. Amnesty International **advocates** the cause for human rights.
2. Martin Luther King, Jr. was a great **advocate** of civil rights.

A899

adj.—1. probable 2. feasible
1. After weeks of trying to determine what or who was raiding the chicken coop, the farmer came up with a **plausible** explanation.
2. After scrimping and saving for a decade, it was now **plausible** to send his daughter to college.

A900

adj.—1. having the characteristics of an island 2. narrow-minded, provincial
1. After walking along the entire perimeter and seeing that the spit of land was actually **insular**, we realized it was time to build a boat.
2. His **insular** approach to education makes him a pariah among liberals.

BLANK CARDS
To Make Up
Your Own Questions

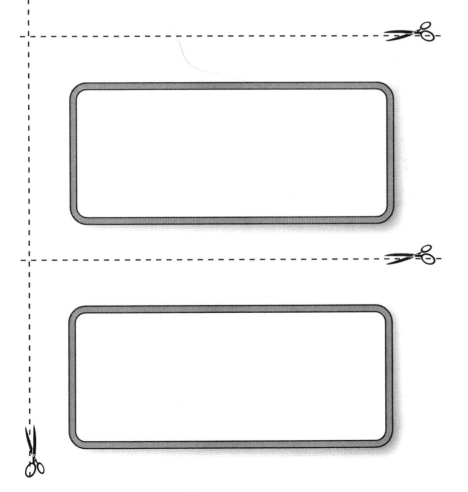

CORRECT ANSWERS

for

Your Own Questions

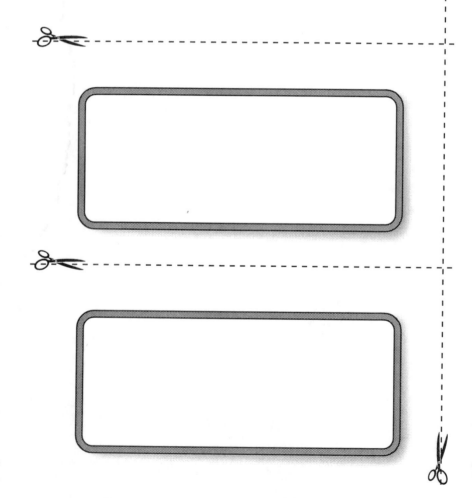

Blank Cards for
Your Own Questions

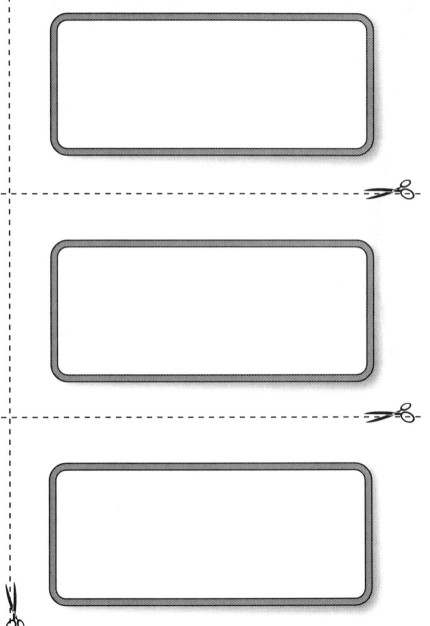

Correct Answers

Blank Cards for
Your Own Questions

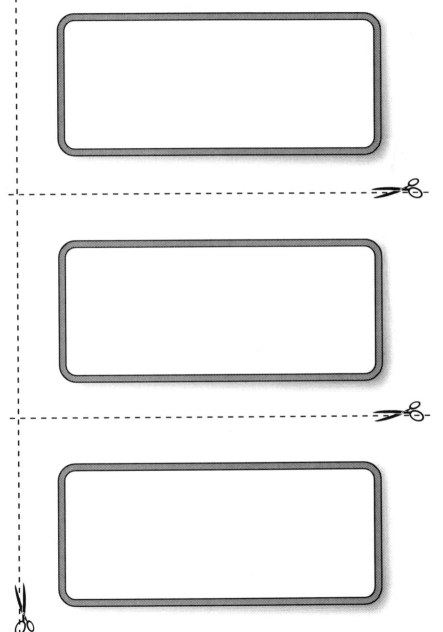

Correct Answers

Blank Cards for *Your Own Questions*

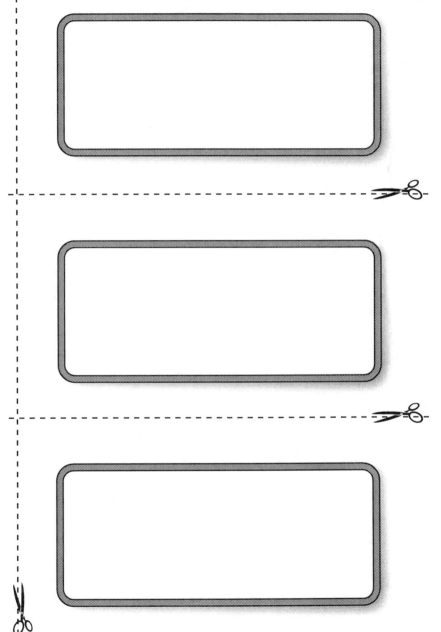

Correct Answers

Blank Cards for
Your Own Questions

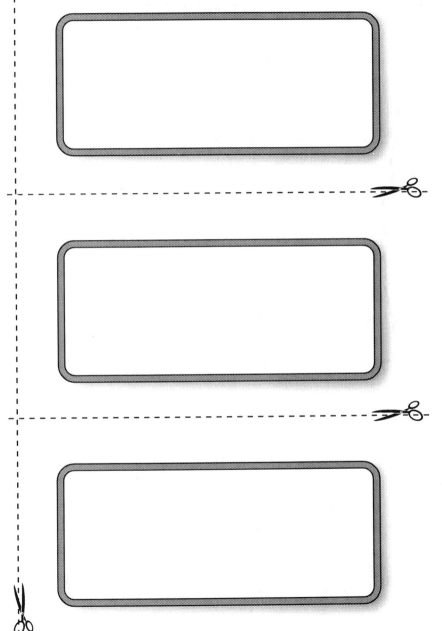

Correct Answers

Blank Cards for
Your Own Questions

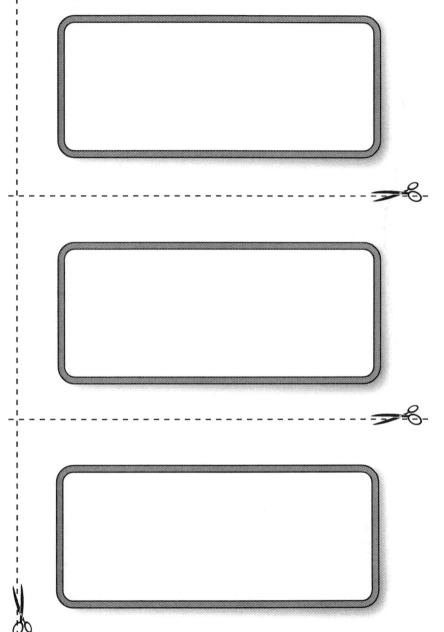

Correct Answers

Blank Cards for
Your Own Questions

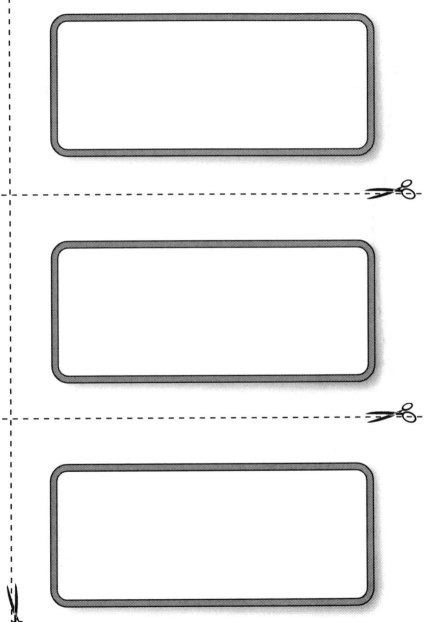

Correct Answers

Blank Cards for
Your Own Questions

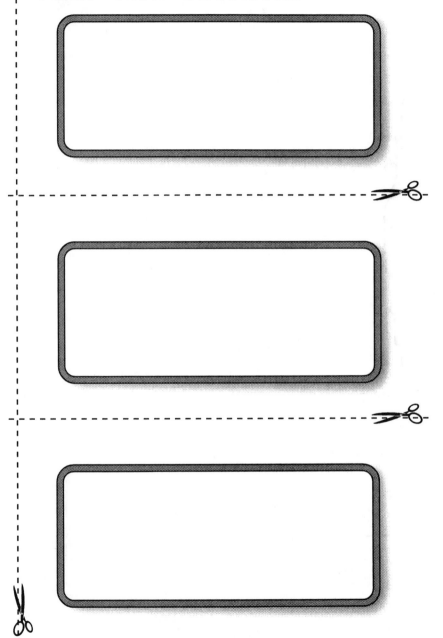

Correct Answers

Blank Cards for
Your Own Questions

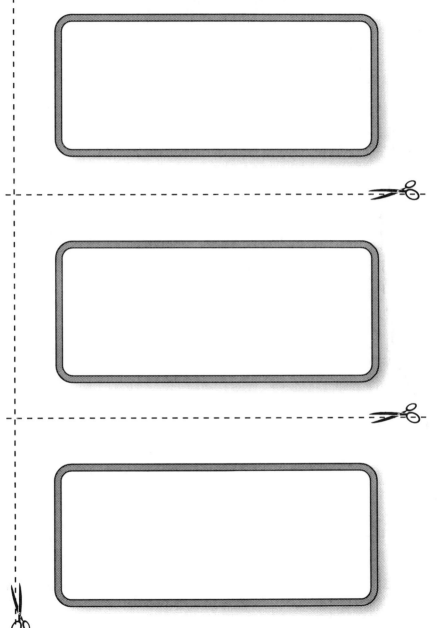

Correct Answers

Blank Cards for
Your Own Questions

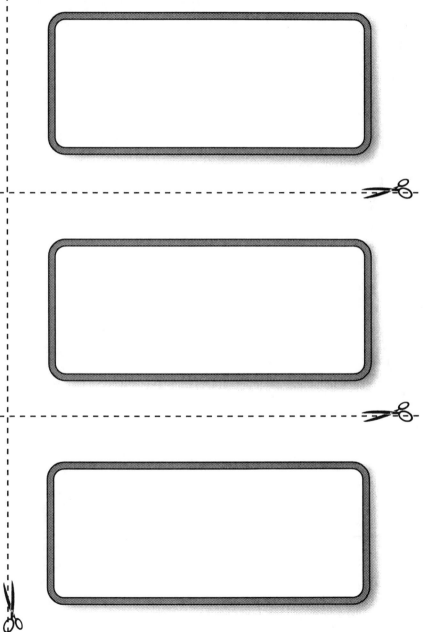

Correct Answers

Blank Cards for
Your Own Questions

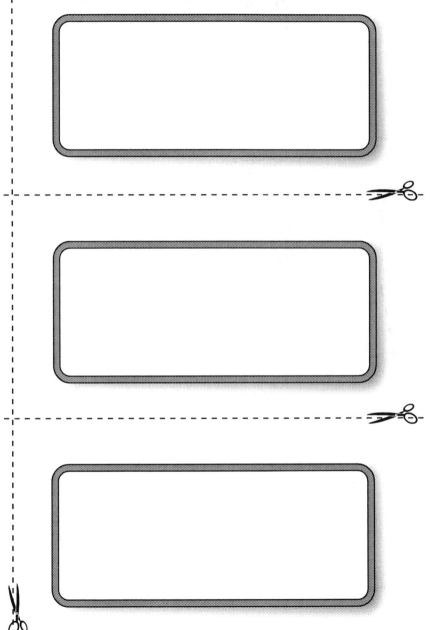

Correct Answers

Blank Cards for
Your Own Questions

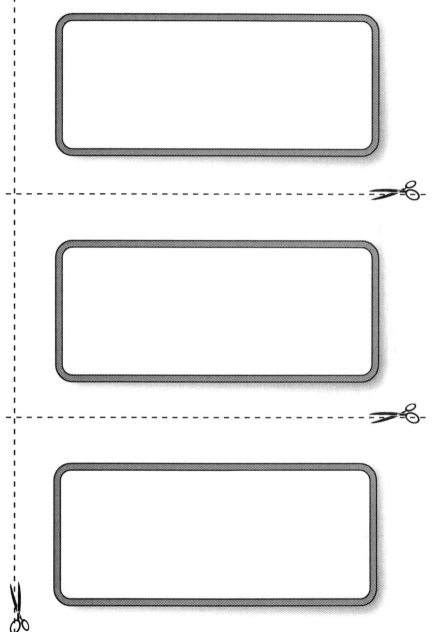

Correct Answers

Blank Cards for
Your Own Questions

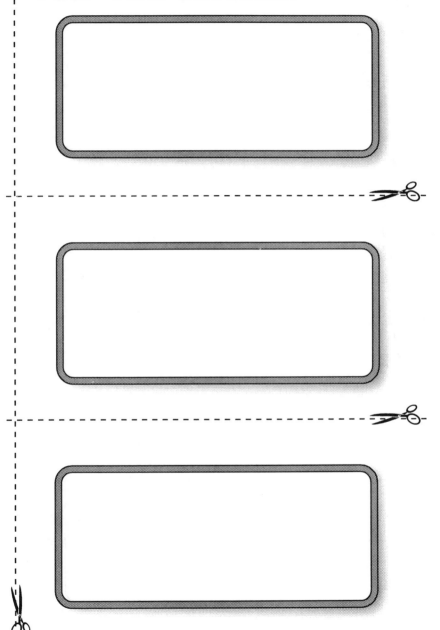

Correct Answers

Blank Cards for
Your Own Questions

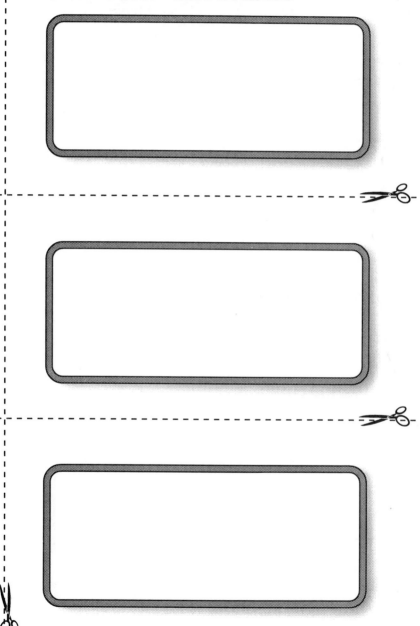

Correct Answers

Blank Cards for
Your Own Questions

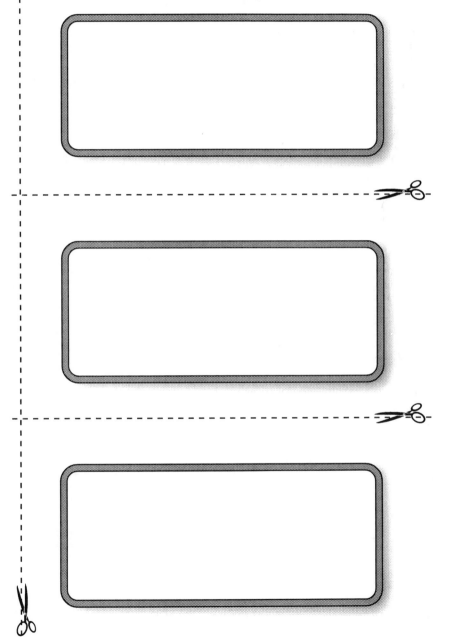

Correct Answers

Blank Cards for
Your Own Questions

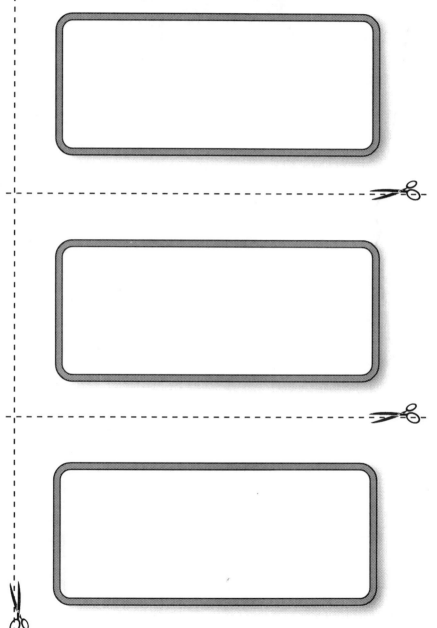

Correct Answers

Blank Cards for
Your Own Questions

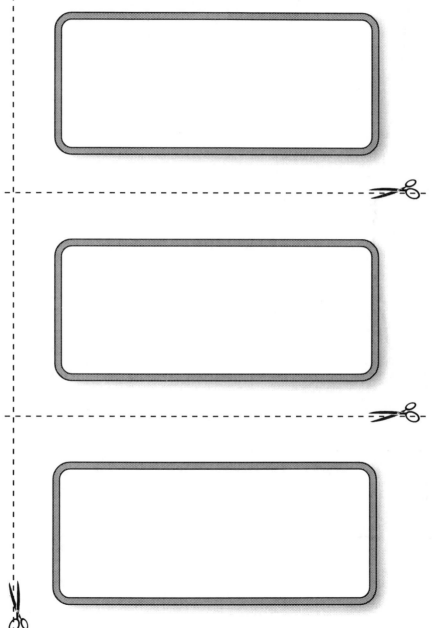

Correct Answers

Blank Cards for *Your Own Questions*

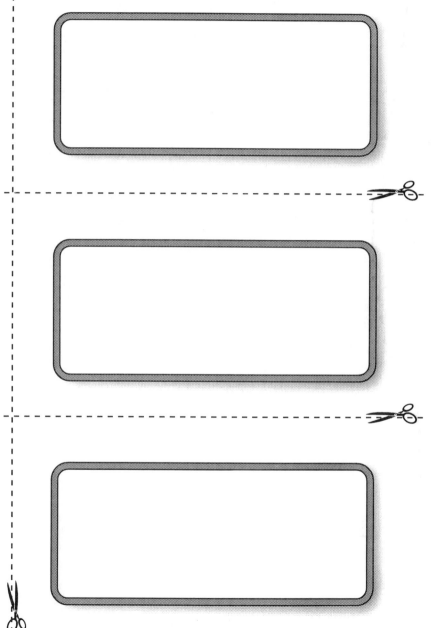

Correct Answers

Blank Cards for
Your Own Questions

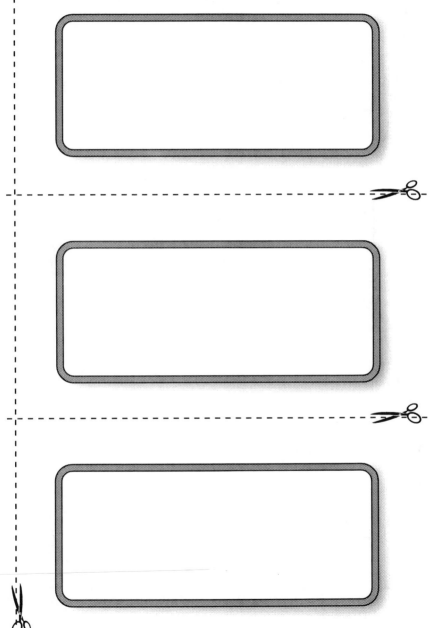

Correct Answers

Blank Cards for
Your Own Questions

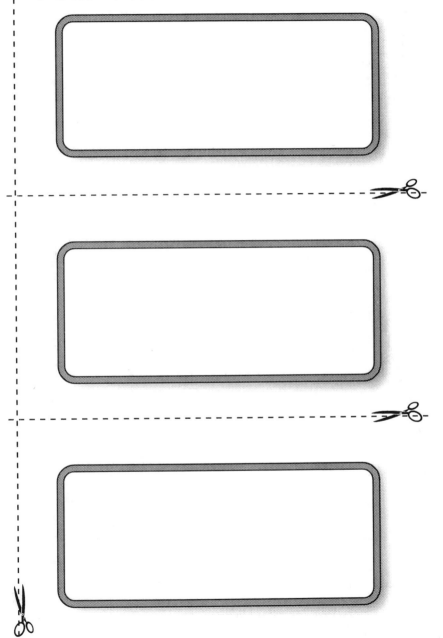

Correct Answers

INDEX

unruly, 95
unwonted, 371
upshot, 92
urbane, 312
usurpation, 706
usury, 532
utopia, 39
vacillation, 554
vacuous, 689
vagabond, 484
vagrant, 855
valance, 56
valiant, 318
valid, 580
valor, 463
vantage, 242
vaunted, 27
vehement, 687
velocity, 130
vendetta, 115
venerate, 245
venue, 53
veracious, 193
verbatim, 646
verbose, 89
versatile, 736
vertigo, 777
vex, 644
viable, 879
vigor, 651
vilify, 117

vindicate, 648
virtuoso, 431
virulent, 492
viscous, 85
vital, 26
vivacious, 665
vogue, 2
volatile, 557
voluble, 84
vulnerable, 720
waft, 150
waive, 457
wane, 314
wanton, 565
warrant, 194
welter, 23
wheedle, 649
whet, 151
whimsical, 438
wither, 199
wooden, 76
workaday, 75
wrath, 714
wretched, 894
wry, 668
xenophobia, 1
yoke, 281
yore, 29
zealot, 71
zenith, 863
zephyr, 561